Cultural Kaizen

The story of how simple concepts can transform an organization's culture, engagement and bottom-line.

Paul W. Swaney III

ISBN: 1475284519
ISBN-13: 978-1475284515

DEDICATION

To Amber, for dealing with me spending three hours a night on the computer after being at the plant for twelve.

To Joe, for believing this would work before anyone else did.

CONTENTS

ACKNOWLEDGMENTS

I would like to thank the following people for their contributions to my life

Darryl Bradley	Thanks for your firm handshake and warm smile on our first meeting.
Dennis Bowman	For teaching me how to build a team through your example.
Dereck Cardinale	Captain 5S…need I say more.
Earl Totty	For letting me bounce cultural ideas off your head over and over again.
Jack Castelli	For our discussions on why throughput is more important than productivity.
Jamie Flinchbaugh	For writing The Hitchhiker's Guide to Lean.
Jody Moffett	Giving me assignments that you knew I could handle before I did.
Joe Quilan	Thanks for setting the pace and growing your team.
Joe Harris	For being a good ear and a friend.
Mike Kicinski	For teaching me the right and wrong way to lead the troops.
Paul Firmin	For teaching me there is a "Big Daddy" in all of us.
Phil Kirby	For asking me questions that I didn't even know I wanted the answer to.
Sergio Lopez	For stepping up when we needed you.
Shy Handy	To this day, ours was the best working relationship I ever had. I learned a great deal from you.
Tim Kline	For helping me grow spiritually and always being there for me.

INTRODUCTION

As I look back over the last several years of my life, I have made a few key mistakes.

1. I initially thought my technical skills would propel me through my career.

Having been a manager for over a decade, I can tell you that nothing is further from the truth once you leave the individual contributor role. Working through people is challenging and no amount of technical skills will prepare you for this role. To take it one step further, it is an *entirely* different skillset managing people. Yet, most of us are appointed to management positions because of our technical competency. I still fight the urge to ask only technical questions when I am interviewing a prospective manager.

2. I thought that work environment was not a factor in a person's happiness.

I used to be of the belief that there were happy people and unhappy people. Happy people would be happy regardless of their job or life circumstance; conversely, unhappy people would never be able to find happiness.

Then I got exposed to the effects of negative organizational culture.

There are, in fact, places so miserable that people can hardly bear their life. I could finally sympathize with the many people that "hated their jobs." A person's occupational life is one of the most important determinants of their happiness or lack thereof. People stay in these organizations for various reasons. Some stay for financial compensation, some stay for fear of change, and some stay for other reasons.

A positive organizational culture is key in developing the conditions required for people to be happy, productive, and effective. There is *no* organizational culture that is right for all people; however, there are *some* organizational cultures that are right for hardly any people.

What Does Lean/Kaizen Have To Do With This?

I am absolutely convinced that a lean transformation is the number one way a company, in any industry, can improve their organizational culture. If lean did nothing else but effect the culture, your results would improve significantly. I can't quantify the amount, but I know, from experience, that if you improve associate morale, you will improve productivity in all areas.

There are several reasons that lean is so effective in improving culture.

1. Lean engages the front-line associate.

Other improvement philosophies require an intensive amount of formal education before you can start utilizing the improvement tools. Lean allows you to very quickly have training on simple concepts; these concepts allow the team to see results quickly. Once the front-line associates see the power that they have over their own destiny, the effects are amazing. Your manager's time will be compounded. The problem will literally become: "I don't have time to implement the average ideas. I only have time for the really good ones."

2. Lean creates a common goal for the team

Make no mistakes about it: a week-long kaizen event is a challenging experience for any person. I have been involved in many week-long kaizens and they all have been challenging in their own way. Having the management and the front-line team rally around a singular sense of purpose will create a bond between the two. By taking a traditional management task -- improving the process -- and allowing collaborative thinking between the line associate and management, you will break down barriers in your organization.

Lean Is Not About The Tools; It's About The People

Any manager can go to Google and type in the word lean; you will get thousands of pages of information regarding the different lean tools that were used in various transformation attempts. The key isn't learning the tools; the key is using a system to engage the people. The mentality has to change before the results will change.

1. THE EFFECTS OF A NEGATIVE CULTURE

"Come on, come on! Send! Finally." For some reason, unbeknownst to me, my network always lagged after hitting the send button on the end-of-shift report to my peers and site leadership. I said cursory good-byes to my team and genuine ones to my production assistant, Ty; he was the only bright spot that existed within the night shift management. I basically ran to my high mileage SUV and proceeded to exit the parking lot and drive - one state away - to my bed. I can't conceivably call it a house because I would only get about four-and-a-half hours of sleep before driving back for yet another exercise in futility.

It was about 7:00 am when I hit the button on the automatic garage door opener. As I unbuckled my seatbelt, I discovered the aromatherapy of bacon grease coupled with hot maple syrup and butter. I gave, what my wife, Nichole, coined, a "less than 50% smile." As a former cheerleader, she took personal responsibility for pumping me up when I had a bad day. Unfortunately, this was becoming the standard instead of the exception. I polished off my blueberry pancakes, kissed Nichole good night, and jumped into bed for my nap.

As I was driving down the turnpike to go back to work, something hit me. I had been in my role for over a year and I was totally frustrated. Uncontrollably, I started crying and I just couldn't bear going back in. I loathed my boss, Tony, and everything he stood for. He was condescending to me in every way possible. He was playing the other two managers on my shift and me against each other. This mentality between second line managers was ubiquitous. Everyone was at each other's throat and in ninja-style competition. This type of behavior was encouraged and even praised. The more negative performance management documents that I wrote because my front-line team hadn't hit their productivity numbers, the better my superiors received me. The more production that I was able to squeeze out of my team by riding their backs throughout the shift, the better congratulatory email I received from the site leader. What was really starting to eat me up inside was that I was good at it; I was ranked the top new manager on site. I had always been good at playing the proverbial game, but in about year I had terminated thirty people. I don't know if the rabbit hole goes this deep, but it almost seemed to be a positive thing when you terminated an associate for not hitting quality or productivity metrics.

Slight Digression

The company I worked for was in the middle of a lean transformation. This lean system is one that I have coined a "check-the-box-system." For example, you want to have front-line associates on the team of a week-long kaizen event; this company would have one on a 10-person team. "Check!" It is 5S rollout time. "Check!" Look at our new kanban system that helps us pull material (at the expense of a ten percent throughput reduction). "Check!"

You get the idea.

During the first kaizen event that I led, I poured my heart and soul into improving one of the most manual processes in the building. We spent the first day and a half mapping out the process while being coached by a Japanese sensei from a well renowned consulting company. We were try-storming like crazy on day three and four; on day five we all stayed late to finalize the remaining changes. We were so proud of hitting our target metrics that were set as stretch goals. I think I got a grand total of twelve hours of sleep during that week, but after all of that effort...the change died. The culture of the site was so bad that no one would embrace the change. I had hand selected line associates from the correct departments to help drive the changes, but it was just not enough to overcome years of bad programming.

Back To My Road Trip

So, there I was about seven miles from work and I called off with a personal day. I had never in my life felt this way before. I had always prided myself on being an excited, motivated, and energetic person; the culture that was omnipresent at this organization had left me a shell of a human being.

I made a U-turn and suddenly the tears were gone. I never let Nichole know that my tears were directly catalyzed by the impending doom that was the last five miles of the turnpike. I knew she would understand, but she isn't the type of person who is going to sit down next to you and rationalize your problems. She is more of a fix-it girl.

I should have seen this coming: the next day my wife had made me an appointment with a psychiatrist. This only led me to further have self-doubt and fear about my career and home life. Was I a failure? Why is this happening to me? I was scared and, worst of all, had no plan to get out of this mess.

Leadership Learnings: People are not the soft side of business. They are the **only** *side of business. When you boil everything down to where it needs to be, all you have are people.*

2. THE THERAPIST AND THE RECRUITER

We weren't speaking while we were driving over to the appointment that Nichole had scheduled for me. I wasn't exactly mad at her for scheduling the impromptu visit, but I cannot safely say that I was thrilled. I had never seen a psychiatrist before and at this point it seemed about a million miles from ideal, but the constant crying and self-loathing behavior was far from what any reasonable person could consider normal.

Whenever there was silence between us, Nichole felt it necessary to fill that dead air.

"So, Dr. Kitari is just going to be asking you some questions…I think. I don't think it will be that big of a deal; hopefully it will be quick and we can get some lunch before you have to go back to work. Are you going to speak to me today?"

"Yes." I responded begrudgingly, "Just give me some space right now… I'm having a tough time at work."

Dr. Kitari's office was nestled into a small shopping center next to the local mall. I signed myself in at the front desk and had a seat amidst the sea of unfamiliar faces and waited for my name to get called. It hardly seemed like where I was supposed to be in my life: I mean, how did I end up here? What had changed in my life to turn me from the happy, life of the party guy to a bitter person who was angry almost all of the time?

"Good afternoon!" Dr. Kitari said. She was a middle aged Asian-Indian woman with a mild accent.

I smirked casually at her and said, "Hello."

I was rather embarrassed at the fact that I had received a "referral" from my wife. I had no idea she even knew to call the number on the back of the insurance card to get an authorization before she scheduled an appointment.

"What seems to be the problem?"

"Well, my wife made me this appointment…I am trying to manage through my problems as best as I can."

"Ok," said Dr. Kitari. "What would your wife say is the reason you are here?"

The List as She Saw It

"Hmmm…that is an interesting question. She would probably rattle off the following:

He calls off of work because he doesn't want to go.
He cries on the way to work.
He is angry most of the time.
He sleeps all day during his time off.
He has lost all of his interest in socializing with our friends.
Things that used to give him joy suddenly do not any longer.
He doesn't spend time with our son."

"That is pretty much what she told me."

Dr. Kitari scribbled some notes onto her pad and looked pensively at them for a brief moment.

"Have you ever thought about suicide or made a plan?"

I started to tear up and responded with a reluctant, "Yes, I have."

Dr. Kitari scribbled some additional notes; I think it is required for a psychiatrist to scribble between questions. I can't be sure, but it all seemed very staged.

"So, do you know why you are so unhappy?"

The Power of a Negative Culture

"That is simple: my job is sucking the life out of me."

Again, the scribbling continued. "What part of your job is making you unhappy?"

I responded, with what I thought was a clever quip, "It's not my job that is making me unhappy; I am making me unhappy. My job is just putting me in an environment where attaining happiness is very difficult."

Dr. Kitari made some additional notes, but commented, "You are avoiding the question. What is difficult about the job? There is no right or wrong answer."

I proceeded to give her the following list:

1. Management is encouraged to disregard the importance of the front-line employee.
2. There is a cut-throat, zero-sum game, competitive nature that exists among managers.
3. Management is encouraged not to trust front-line employees.
4. Performance is managed with mostly sticks and very few carrots.
5. A healthy amount of workplace fun is discouraged.
6. General air of negativity throughout the site.
7. Copious amounts of micromanagement present and expected.

I realized at this point that I had lost her. I think she expected me to say I was being harassed or I was having performance problems. Quite the contrary existed. I was the number one rated manager on site and I was totally miserable. I received daily emails from upper management praising how successful my improvement projects and shift performance were. Again… totally miserable! She wrote me a script for two different antidepressants, an anti-anxiety drug, and some sleeping pills. At the behest of my wife, I did start the regimen of medicine; I knew she was sincerely worried about me and she hoped this would be the start of regaining her happy husband.

The Phone Call

Let's flash forward two weeks. I had now been immersed in my dual-diagnosis, of major depressive disorder and anxiety, and subsequent prescriptions and was doing somewhat better at dealing with the environment I had been sentenced to endure. My production assistant, Ty, and I were getting ready for the start of our shift.

"Ty, make sure you staff line 'A' with enough people tonight and make sure that you stay on top of them. I don't want our rates to slip this close to review time." Managers tend to have short memories-I was becoming fond of exploiting this fact.

"You got it boss," said Ty. "I will stick Derrick on the line as operator; he will put up big numbers."

This is the drill that Ty and I went through night after night. He was one of the most effective junior managers I had ever met. There wasn't anything I could throw at him that he couldn't handle with ease. It is the best working relationship that I have ever had; it was the eye that existed within the cultural hurricane that was spinning around us. I taught him a lot and learned even more from him.

After about thirty minutes of this back and forth between us, we had the shift ready to go for the evening. Then suddenly, my cellphone rang. I didn't recognize the number on my caller ID; usually I would send something to voicemail during work, but I decided to pick it up.

"Hello."

The unfamiliar voice responded, "Hi! This is Clark from UGA Recruiting. I have a client who is looking for an experienced operations manager to run a small plant. Might you be interested?"

I had about a thousand thoughts in my head during that short phone call. *Should I be making a move? I really hate it here, but the money is good and the benefits are great. Can I handle more responsibility? Could I really run my own site?*

I quickly gathered myself together and exclaimed, "Absolutely. Can you call me back tomorrow around 8 am? I currently work the night shift."

"Sure, I will talk to you then. Could you forward me an updated copy of your resume in the meantime?"

That was the fastest nightshift I ever had at work. I could literally taste the freedom.

3. FIRST DAY, NEW JOB

I drove my Toyota down the hill from the hotel we were staying at and turned onto the interstate. I hopped off about three exits down and waited at the light to turn into the main entrance of the plant.

Flashback

A vision hopped through my head of the interview that got me here. Waiting in a small conference room at the corporate headquarters, I pondered my resume for about five minutes. *What kind of presentation was I going to make to the executives that would be handing me the third degree?*

I was astounded to talk to a human resources business partner first. I knew from that moment that this was not going to be a standard interview. This went on for about eight hours. I cannot remember exactly what was asked of me until the vice president of operations asked me, "What is your strategy for running a plant?"

I took a longer pause than I normally would take in an interview and finally answered, "I want to put systems in place to work myself out of a job."

He looked at me quite a bit puzzled and said, "How do you make that happen?"

I thought about how miserable I was in my current role and I looked over the table and said to him, "I know how to create an environment to make people want to come to work and give it their all."

I realize that was a bold statement, but, if I knew nothing else, I know what a negative work environment is. My thinking was that I would do exactly the opposite of that and we would be ok.

Back to the Stoplight

So there I sat after moving my entire family across the country, waiting for the stoplight to turn so I could show up to my new life. It finally flickered from red to green. I slowly accelerated to the gate surrounding the plant. "Good morning!" the guard, Marcos, exclaimed.

Marcos was about thirty five years old and had a permanent smile plastered about his face. I would come to appreciate his ever present smiles over the next several months. The consistency and predictability of our "running conversations" made driving through the gate that much easier.

Leadership Learnings: A lighthouse always burns with the same level of intensity and consistency. Be that constant in your team's life. Your team will grow to appreciate those traits in you.

Back to the Interview

"Do you have any questions for me?" the vice president asked.

I am accustomed to getting that question in every single interview I have ever been a part of. "Yes, as a matter of fact, I do," I retorted quickly. "Why is the plant manager position vacant?"

The executive paused and then said, "Look, I don't want to discourage you; the plant needs serious help. We let the previous plant manager go."

He paused for a few additional seconds and continued, "The culture at the plant is atrocious; there is zero buy-in to any programs we put in place, productivity is down significantly, customers are unsatisfied, *and* we just had a string of injuries over the last few months. I finally had to let the plant manager go. The production manager was offered the job, but he was afraid to step into a new role for fear of being fired."

"Ok, that makes sense. I have one more question and then I should be finished."

Again, the executive looked puzzled. "What is your question?"

I paused for a few moments and asked, "Will I have 100% support for my methodology of improving the plant culture?"

I think my frankness slightly offended my future manager, but I knew I could not mince words if I was going to uproot my family and take on a challenge like this. I also knew that if he was being this vocal about the state of affairs of the site, it would be significantly worse than he was communicating.

"If you can turn the plant around, you will have my 100% total support. Quite frankly, my job is depending on it, but I have dozens of other plants in my span of control."

Back to Marcos

Based on the conversation I had with the vice president of operations, I had not expected the warm welcome that Marcos had given me. He verified my ID and proceeded to let me onto the facility. I drove up to the site and parked my car in the employee parking lot. As I walked past the front entrance, I noticed a curious sight: immediately next to the two disabled parking spots was a sign that read: Plant Manager. That sign, coupled with the vice president's statement about the site culture, spoke volumes about how the previous person had run the site. I walked by the sign and shook my head in disbelief. I noticed a few noses pushed up against the glass as I walked into the building, but they quickly returned to their respective computers.

As I entered the lobby I noticed two things. One, the lights were basically off throughout the building. There was some serious need for a spruce up. Two, the sign-in sheet for the plant was blank for the last month or so. I signed my name into the book and rang the bell. Out popped a tall gentleman in his late forties with a company uniform on and a radio coupled to his ear.

"I'm George. I am the production manager here."

"Awesome! Good to meet you," I responded.

George proceeded to tell me that he had my office prepared and that all my onboarding paperwork was ready to go to Human Resources. I sat down in my new office for a few minutes to get my bearings.

I called George's office. "Can you get the management team in here around noon for a meet and greet? Also, can you point me in the direction of a good pizza place? I want to go pick up some food."

George sounded a bit puzzled or confused; he finally said, "Sure. we will be there at 12:30 in the conference room! The best pizza in town is from a place called Pacino's. Do you want me to have purchasing pick it up?"

"It's ok George, I will get the food. I still work for a living." *Did I really say that – that very same lame line I had heard all my managers in the military regurgitate?* I could hardly believe those words came out of my mouth.

A few hours later, I drove down to pick up the pizza for the team and realized that I had absolutely no idea of what I was going to say during our first meeting. I would have a dozen or so people looking to me for answers and I hadn't even been out to the floor yet.

4. PIZZA, PROCESS, ORG CHART

It was about 11:45 am and I was pulling back through the gate with five large pizzas of assorted varieties, a cooler full of sodas, and a cake. Marcos waved me through the gate again and I proceeded to drive up to the plant. Again I bypassed the plant manager parking space for a spot with the rest of the team and, again, I felt puzzled thinking about whether it was the previous manager or the one before who erected this totem of disrespect to the front-line associate.

Pizza Time

It was 12:00 now and I was bringing the food into the plant's conference room. Sara, who turned out to be the plant's health and safety specialist, rushed over to give me a hand with the food and proceeded to spread it out across the tables in the back of the room.

"Thank you!" I said.

She smiled and looked down. I would later come to find that she was afraid of losing her job because there were three injuries last year and she had not been completing the required number of safety reports and finalizing the required work instructions in company format.

Everyone sat down at the U-shaped tables. I purposely chose to not sit in the front of the room. I shook hands with the remaining members of the team that I had not met yet.

Meet Your Plant Management Team

Steve was the plant logistics manager. He had a firm handshake and although he seemed a bit nervous about meeting his new boss for the first time, I could tell immediately that he was a strong leader with a good heart.

Frankie was the plant maintenance manager. He was a very quiet phlegmatic type, but according to George, nothing ever got fixed until Frankie showed up. People weren't exactly excited about the pace of his work, but the results were always top notch when he did deliver. I liked him immediately. If anyone has ever watched the TV show *Friends*, he had a classic "work-laugh" and he always seemed to be in good spirits.

Kellen was the plant's process engineer. He didn't technically report to me, because he was a part of the corporate process-engineering group. As a matter of proxy, he was in effect, our plant's engineer. Kellen was one of the smartest engineers I had ever met, possibly too smart. He was a chemical engineer with a 3.9 GPA and the president of the engineering honor society. He was a six-sigma master black belt and he was actively pursuing a graduate certificate in operations management. This was a guy you wanted on your team. Kellen and I hit it off immediately; I could see that he had a clear picture of how he wanted the plant to work, but no buy-in from any of the other team members.

Johnny was the first shift production supervisor. Every time I looked at him all I could think about was the movie *Shrek*, "I'm an ogre!!" Johnny stood about 6'4" tall and weighed about 260. I genuinely think that some of his team was afraid of him at first. When I first met him, I never would have guessed that Johnny would become my greatest asset for what I was about to do to change the culture of the plant.

Henry was the second shift production supervisor. He shook my hand slightly begrudgingly. He was another phlegmatic type and I think that the previous plant manager and he were close.

Plant Organization Chart

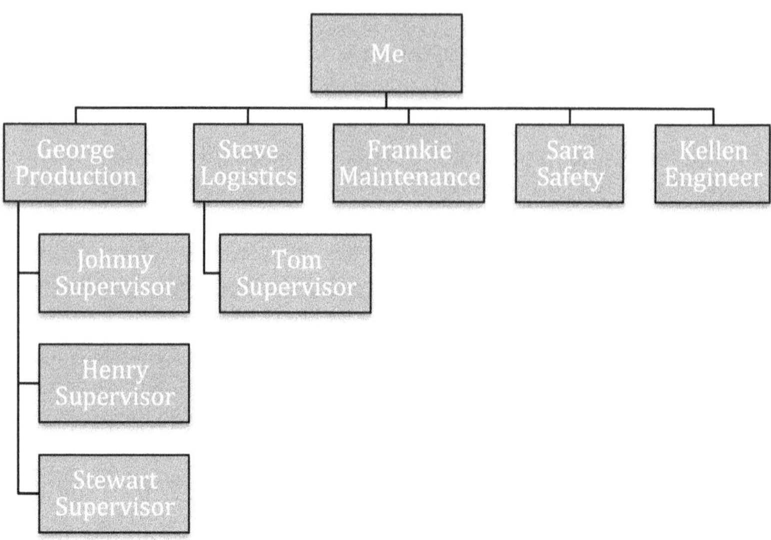

Twenty Questions

So, doing as my normal style has led me to believe is best, I started asking some questions. "So, George, what products do you make here?" George proceeded to look flabbergasted and slightly offended at the prospect of his new manager having no idea what products were being produced and distributed from our site. Steve, the logistics manager, smirked slightly; I thought he could tell what I was doing.

George quickly retorted, "We make a special type of plastic resin, of different grades, that we ship out in either drums, fifty pound bags, 2000 pound bulk bags, or by the truckload that is a raw material for many other plants. Johnny is the first shift supervisor and the resin manager. Also, we make a solvent-based contact adhesive for application on printed circuit boards; it gets shipped out in caulk-type tubes or drums. Henry is the production supervisor for that process."

"Very good!" I responded. "Do we make a superior product?"

George proudly said, "Yes, we have the best product in the marketplace. Our service level leaves plenty to be desired, but our product keeps our customers loyal."

I smiled at George; this was my personal way of letting him off of the hot seat. I genuinely wanted to ask more questions of the team, but I could already tell that, as a whole, they were nervous enough.

"Johnny, what kind of process is making resin?"

Johnny started to answer and George quickly cut him off, "We are batchy for our mixing and reaction process; I would consider our packaging a pseudo-continuous process."

Process Manufacturing 101

Batch Process: Production where the finished good is created in different stages over a series of work stations.

Examples of batch processing include: bakeries, paint manufacturing, pharmaceuticals, and adhesives.

Continuous Process: Production method used to manufacture finished goods or process materials without interruption.

Examples of continuous processing include: refineries, chemical plants, pulp & paper, and power plants.

Johnny looked irritated and embarrassed. I smiled at him in a vain attempt to set him at ease. Even though I didn't know that Johnny would end up being my keystone leadership team member in about three months, there was no reason for me to make him uncomfortable.

"So Sara, would you be able to get me the proper safety equipment to start working on the floor with the team by Wednesday morning?"

Sara looked like she had just seen a ghost. I had just barbequed my first sacred cow. Apparently the previous plant manager had told the team that it was a terrible example for the management to be co-mingling with the line associates. The direct quote was, "Managers are managers and workers are workers; we tell them what to do and we do not do it for them." I had also just opened my first can of worms.

Leadership Learnings: Do not create a separation mentality in your organization. All people, regardless of position, have an important function in every organization.

Sara responded, "Sir, I don't think that's a good idea. What if you get hurt on the floor? You haven't been trained."

I nodded my head. "Sara, that is an absolutely valid possibility. The team on the floor will keep me safe. They have the most experience running the process and know more about making plastic resin than anyone on site. I will shadow them and learn. We cannot begin to improve until we respect the team on the floor's position in this facility. They print the money that pays our salaries, not vice-versa. I will take full, personal responsibility for my personal safety while I am working the floor. I will not drive a forklift since I am not certified. Does that seem amicable to you?"

Sara responded hesitantly, "Yes, but I don't understand what this will do for you."

I quietly responded to her, "All I know right now is that I know absolutely nothing about the people, process, or products that we manufacture and distribute to our customers. If I get on the floor, I will close that gap much quicker than sitting in an office."

There were many mixed reactions coming from the team as we finished our lunch. I got a few questions about my background and I tried to downplay it as much as possible. I would quickly ask another question to take the focus off me as quickly as possible. The team definitely had some growth that needed to occur, but we had the foundation of a world-class manufacturing organization.

"Ok team, it was nice meeting you all today. I will be out on the floor for the next week or so asking questions and trying to learn. Let me know if you need anything, but you guys are the heart and soul of this site. You don't need me to tell you how to do your jobs for you.

"Tomorrow, we go to the gemba and batch with the front-line team!" I got a few puzzled looks. For the most part, I think the team thought I was a bit crazy.

5. DIRECT TASK CULTURE DRIVING

I rolled up to Marcos at around 5:00 am the next morning. I opened a box of local made doughnuts and let him have his pick. The subtle smile very quickly turned into an ear-to-ear grin.

He responded, "Thanks very much. I never got the royal treatment from the last guy with the parking spot."

I proceeded to drive into the plant and, yet again, I parked amidst the now significantly less number of cars. I liked to come to a manufacturing site on the back shift, because you can always tell how a plant is really running when no one is paying close attention.

I went down to my office and I saw a neat stack of folded Nomex® coveralls adorned by a full-face respirator, Kevlar® gloves, chemical gloves, hard hat, safety glasses, steel toe boots, and a safety cutter. Next to the pile was a short scribbled note that read:

Make sure to wear the required personal protective equipment and try not to get hurt ☺
-Sara

I think this was her way of shaking hands in the midst of what I perceived to be a difficult transition for most of the site. I put on all of the gear and proceeded to walk out onto the manufacturing floor. As I passed through the break room, I noticed that there was an associate sleeping in the corner of the room on a lunch bench. I exited onto the floor and quickly found an associate to talk to.

"Hi. I'm new here. Can you do me a favor and talk to the associate sleeping? Can you wake him up, please?" We talked for a second longer and the associate, Doug, said that the sleeper, Aaron, works two jobs and picks up side work to keep his kids fed.

Leadership Learnings: "In the absence of information, our minds get filled with devils instead of angels." Don't make assumptions until you know the facts.

"Wow. Just tell him that the new guy is coming on site and wanted him to be awake in case of an emergency."

"Is he going to be fired?" Doug asked cautiously.

"No." I said, "It's not time to make a big deal out of things. I'm still trying to get my bearings and learn what you all are doing here to service the customer."

Doug looked perplexed; I told him not to worry about it for the moment.

I walked around the facility for another forty five minutes or so. I paced myself and introduced myself to operators. I would get random joking comments such as, "What are you going to do with that respirator?"

I would slyly reply, "In about 15 minutes I am going to go make a batch with the team." The responses to my statement ranged from laughter to puzzlement and even the occasional negative or scorning comment.

At about 6:30 am, I headed into the reaction area and started introducing myself to people. I spotted one operator in particular that, I believed, could be my wingman for the day. Dave greeted me with 110% of the enthusiasm that I expected based on the vice president of operations' assessment of the organizational culture.

"Good morning!" he said. "Welcome to the first shift reaction team. We're the best shift in the plant, but you already know that."

"Nice to meet you, Dave!" I instantly mirrored his enthusiasm; I knew that a positive culture was like a virus. I didn't want this one to die in the petri dish.

"Dave, would you mind taking a few hours out of your day to show me how to do your job? I'd like it even better if you could mentor and coach me while I am doing the work."

He responded quickly and even more enthusiastically, "I thought you'd never ask. This is going to be the best shift EVER!"

Dave spent the next several hours walking me through every single step of the process. He was extremely careful to annotate where I needed to wear my full-face respirator and which particular type of protective gloves were required with each type of chemical we were adding. He quietly pointed out that we had some spectators paying attention to what we were doing. I told him that we didn't want to draw attention to ourselves and that I wanted to keep learning as long as it wasn't disruptive.

He agreed to continue. We finished loading the lead reactor after about two hours and I switched on the controls per Dave's direction. I have to admit that I got a little bit scared when the vacuum system turned on and the temperature gauge started to climb to 400° F. It leveled off abruptly and we proceeded to go fire up the tertiary reactor system.

Several more hours passed and we started to talk about more benign topics. Dave had almost twenty years with the company and two kids in high school. He was a total sports fanatic on all fronts and liked to homebrew beer right before football season. He had it timed so he would be drinking his home brew during most of the NFL season.

This went back and forth for several minutes and I could tell that he was starting to get frustrated.

"So why are you really out here with me today? I've never seen a manager on the floor for more than like fifteen minutes at a time," he asked in the most non-threatening way possible.

"I spend a lot of time learning on the floor; it's what I do. I come out on the floor and have the experts show me the ropes."

Dave looked even more confused. I wanted to say something, but he quickly replied, "We're not the experts; none of us have engineering degrees."

I paused for a brief minute. I could tell where the perception of the bad culture came from. The team here had basically been disenfranchised.

"Let me ask you a question. Who is your favorite football player of all time?"

Dave was about to talk over me he was so excited. "That's easy: Barry Sanders. Barry danced on the field. He was so impressive to watch."

I smiled and responded, "So what school did he attend to get his football degree? It must have been Harvard or Yale since he was one of the best running backs ever."

Dave looked at me like I was crazy. "No, he has a basket-weaving degree or something. He learned how to play football in high school and college."

"Ok," I said. "So he was an expert who never went to school. Kellen, the process engineer, told me he had been here about fifteen months and I've been here a few days. How long have you been running this specific process?"

He looked up at the ceiling for a few seconds and responded, "Fourteen or fifteen years!"

I looked him dead in the eye and retorted, "You and your team in the reaction area have all the experience. Based on the staffing level and age of the site, I'm guessing that it is in excess of a thousand years. Your team lives here in the gemba; gemba is Japanese for 'the real place.' You all are here day-in day-out in 'the real place' and you know exactly what we need to do to make this place a world-class operation. My job is to help you guys do just that, but you will always be the experts. I will basically be your steward."

I shook Dave's hand and wandered back up front for a conference call I had with my new boss. The team was obviously talking about me as I was walking back up to the plant offices. I don't think I had ever wished so much that I knew what someone was saying. I had to work from the assumption that it was positive. If I felt any other way, it would have eaten me from the inside out.

My new cell phone rang just as I was walking into my office…

Leadership Learnings: If you don't genuinely believe that your front-line team has all the answers, you will never have a world-class culture. There will be a mental stop that prevents you from harvesting their ideas, because the belief will be that they will fail. You might be able to sustain small improvements, but you will never reap the 100% engagement that you could have if you would just let go of your hang-ups.

6. THE PHONE CALL

Aftermath

The juxtaposition of my five hour 'Gemba-fest '97' with Dave the operator and the phone call I just had was almost comical in nature. It was certainly worthy of making me think of a series of B movies I had watched over summer vacation while I was in junior-high.

I had been given a list of six metrics for the coming year that had absolutely nothing to do with satisfying any customers. I was also given a list of human resources items that made me throw up in my mouth a little bit!

I sat in my office with my door shut for about thirty five minutes playing the phone call and its specific verbiage back through my head. I had scribbled some shorthand notes onto a yellow sticky note and made some longer notes in an email, but I couldn't wrap my head around this volume of gross conceptual errors. I had had a similar feeling about fifteen years earlier, about three days into training after enlisting in the military.

My buyer's remorse had kicked in and I was considering the ramifications of the decisions I had made. I had moved my family over 2,500 miles across the country. Nichole was not going to be happy; I decided to keep this one to myself.

I made a list of notes in a document on my computer and while I was typing my hands started to shake. I was now nervous, frustrated, and empowered at the same time. I was piecing a plan together to turn this plant around, but it was absolutely polar to what my boss was requesting. I printed out my game plan and taped it to the wall across from my desk so I would see it throughout the day. I smirked a little bit at the sight of my translation of the metrics that were thrust upon me. I felt like those archaeologists who uncovered the Rosetta Stone: using some basic knowledge of lean manufacturing, I restructured my boss's game plan for our site. I changed the goal to create a positive company culture instead of one of mistrust.

Rewind: The Phone Call

I looked at my ringing phone and hesitated slightly before picking up. "Good morning from Minnesota," he said. "It is Devon."

My new vice president of operations was an Eastern European man named Devon Carpenter. Apparently, the back-story is that he was the byproduct of a former executive at a major manufacturing corporation. His parents had earmarked him to be an executive at an early age. He had attended all of the best schools from the time he was three. He was a graduate of an extremely prestigious business and engineering school. I also came to find that the majority of the organization was afraid of him. He had closed five factories in the last four years and had been eyeballing my new home for the last eighteen months. He had discovered that the way to fix a management problem was to close business down. On a percentage basis, the company was making more money; the capital return was higher and the accountants were satisfied. The company was physically making fewer dollars though. He unknowingly was turning the company into a non-profit organization.

"So," stated Devon, "did you get the list of key performance indicators that I emailed to you?"

I remembered reading the subject line of the email, but I had spent my time with Dave figuring out how to start up that machine (and making a new friend). I told him I had added it to my calendar to review. I didn't realize that we would be reviewing today.

"No problem; I know you are still getting settled. Why don't you open it now?"

I opened the single power-point slide and started reviewing. My palms started to sweat.

Devon proceeded to review the list one by one with me. "The safety performance of all the plants is atrocious. The safety director and I have made a commitment to reduce injuries to zero. So, whatever you need to do to make that happen, just let me know."

I could see where this was going. I was getting a set of coffin nails and absolutely zero support.

"The second metric is our productivity target. Our overseas owners mandate this one so I have no control of the number. When we do our budget cycle next year, we should be able to reduce our headcount by at least 10%."

I don't know why I asked when I should have just kept my mouth shut, but I opened it anyways. "Why don't we just sell more instead of cutting heads? It will just alienate our team more and destroy the culture further if they see their friends disappear."

Devon seemed a little bit irritated when he responded. "We are not sales and marketing. We worry about operations costs and the way we make more money is by cutting the budget. If sales increase by 20%, we don't have to cut heads; we will stay 'headcount neutral.'"

That was the last time I would make the mistake of opening my mouth. I now knew that he had a cleverly canned answer for it all.

"The next measure is absolutely the most important one. We have to cut the budget every single year. Our jobs depend on our ability to manage the budget. I know you will get it done."

Again, I had received a target with no plan or system to get me to our goal. I could see that Devon turned his team into bean counters. Dave's respirator looked like it had about 100,000 miles on it. I had left him with my shiny new one after he helped train me. It was blatantly obvious that someone found safety equipment as a way to cut costs.

"Our final major area of improvement is the service level of the plant. The plant is only achieving an A-plus order rate of 60%. If we want to satisfy our customers, we will have to get that up to 90%. Put some systems in place to make that happen."

I sighed to myself and asked, "How do you define an A-plus order?"

I could tell he was waiting for that question by his reply.

"An A-plus order is the synergy of on-time shipment, on-time delivery, order fill rate, pick accuracy, damage free, and invoiced correctly. Our quality director can fill you in more. I just know that the 60% result is not where it needs to be.

"Ok, now we have a few HR items to discuss that were lingering from before the transition period.

"Your plant had three injuries last year and scored significantly below average on the internal safety audit last year. You should probably get a new safety specialist. Sara was a bad hire and not meshing with our culture of continuous improvement. I will give you the ability to use a 20% salary increase to help get a new person in the role.

"Next..."

I gulped while he talked. "Kellen, the process engineer, is not safety focused. He interviewed for the plant manager position, but there is no way he could ever do that job effectively with his safety mindset.

"Finally, George Diaz, the production manager, was placed in his role before I was advanced. He is not an engineer by trade. We must have degreed engineers in the production and plant manager roles."

I had spoken with George during the pizza party and found out that he had worked as an electro-mechanical maintenance technician at another plant for ten years, had finished up his business management degree, and completed an operations management certification. Additionally, he was a sponge for knowledge. His previous plant was collocated with a research and development center. He knew more than most would know about the reactive chemistry associated with the production of our products. It seemed exceptionally dismissive to not give this guy a shot.

Plant Organization Chart: Devon's Hit list

Me
George Production
Steve Logistics
Frankie Maintenance
Sara Safety
Kellen Engineer
Johnny Supervisor
Tom Supervisor
Henry Supervisor
Stewart Supervisor

My direct manager had given me the equivalent of a terrorist hit list. He didn't force my hand, but it was strongly encouraged. I now had an additional goal of running interference and proving that I could unite this team.

I begrudgingly said thank you in the most positive tone I could muster and got off the phone, totally exhausted with frustration.

Back to the Gemba

I left the room after thirty more minutes of contemplating my new "metrics" and proceeded to return to the floor. I shook hands with a few new operators and warehouse personnel, but my primary purpose was again to learn the workflow of the facility. I went to the packaging line and literally just stood there for about two hours making mental notes.

It was time to make my way to the house. I knew that this time next week I had to discuss my plans with the teams.

Leadership Learnings: The continuous improvement mentality was started in the last half of the twentieth century. The assumption was made initially that we would help people simultaneously. Managers have begun to take the easy way out: **I will raise my metrics yearly without improving my processes and hold my team accountable regardless.** *If you don't have a genuine respect for people, you will never have a culture that facilitates true continuous improvement.*

7. THE LEADERSHIP TEAM & THE PLAN

After the call that I just had with my supervisor, it was obvious that I had no time to waste. I went to all of my managers' offices and informed them that I wanted to have a pull-together meeting of the plant leadership team at 2:00 pm. I told George to call in Scott off the night shift so that he could meet with us. Normally I would not have made that kind of request, but this wasn't something that I wanted communicated second-hand.

"George, tell Scott that I will take care of him down the road, but that it is important that we meet today."

George could sense the urgency in my voice. "I'll make sure he gets down to the plant. He is the kind of guy that would want to hear this first-hand. If he's not here I will be telling it to him about seven times anyway."

I had a few hours to kill until the meeting so I threw a few presentation slides together so I could talk more intelligibly about my plan. I felt like all the dotcom start-up companies that I heard about in business school that literally scratched out their business vision on a cocktail napkin. I would be lying if I told anyone that I didn't have doubts about my plan going through my head. I had read *The Machine That Changed The World* about a dozen times, but at this point it was still all theory from the perspective of site leadership. I decided that I would go out and grab a bite to eat for lunch and not attend the regular production meeting. I wanted to convey at least some level of mystique while sharing my plan with the team.

I went to a local Italian restaurant and was being served by a pleasant young Italian woman. I smirked slightly at her and said, "You aren't from around here are you?" She told me that she was from New Jersey and that her family wanted a change of climate about three years ago so they decided to set up shop out here.

I chuckled and said, "Oh nice! I lived in Rahway for a few years, but I have been bouncing around. I just moved here like a month ago. I think I made a career mistake, but hopefully I can salvage it."

She said, "I hope you do. I don't meet many people from out that way." I ordered the spaghetti carbonara and some bruschetta. I polished off my food, said good-bye to the server and made my way back to the plant.

I went in the conference room and powered on the projector to get ready for my meeting. I have to admit that I was feeling a bit twitchy; I still can't tell if that was because of stress or my eight cup a day coffee habit. It was 1:45 pm and I decided to make a quick lap around the plant before sitting down. I always hated talking in front of people and I had never laid out this kind of a structure before, so I needed to burn off some nervous energy.

I had intended to make it out in the plant, but Dave and a friend of his that I hadn't met yet stopped me in the break room.

Dave said, "Hey! I want you to meet Joe. Tell him what you told me about Barry Sanders and a degree in football-ology."

I laughed out loud and then gave Joe the analogy about the difference between learning something in a book and doing it every day.

Joe seemed intrigued, but he carefully asked, "Why did you spend time in the reaction area with Dave? I have been here almost fifteen years and no manager has ever done that. Do you not trust us?"

I understood why he took this as a potential negative; I was just glad that he spoke up. I replied, "Not at all. I wanted to learn what you guys do. I can't learn that unless I'm out there on the floor experiencing it first-hand. You guys have batch cards from our ERP system, but those don't tell the whole story. Only someone like Dave can paint the real picture. Does that make sense?"

He said yes, but he still seemed quite a bit confused or, at a minimum, cautious.

"Guys, I have a meeting to go to with the plant leadership team. We will be talking about a new plan tomorrow morning or the next day."

We said our good-byes and I walked back to the plant conference room. It was already filled with my new team and they seemed anxious. Presumably this was because I called Scott in from the night shift. I shook Scott's hand and introduced myself to him. More so than Joe, he seemed guarded; this was totally understandable since he had only been off of work for about eight hours and we woke him up about four hours into his sleep.

I sat down and decided not to mince words.

"Team, I'm going to be very short and to the point. I think that if we don't make drastic improvements in a very short period of time that they may end up closing our site down."

Most of the room snickered; those who didn't rolled their eyes.

Frankie, the maintenance manager, sarcastically said, "We were all wondering when you were going to figure it out. We are surprised we have lasted this long. We tell the customers we will ship in fourteen days and usually it's twenty or more. The racks are empty 'cause we can't make product fast enough. We have a significant number of product quality issues and a matching number of customer complaints."

Sara chimed in, "We had three injuries last year and one of them was a lost time injury; the poor guy burned a part of his hand. It is going to be a serious workers compensation case."

George further added, "Our productivity is the lowest in the network for all of the products we make and your boss chalks it up to the fact that I don't have an engineering degree."

I paused for about thirty seconds, sighed and replied to the group. "We can fix all that if you guys want! We can be the best site in the network, have no injuries, highest productivity, and cut our lead time in half. I have a plan."

Johnny, who usually didn't say much, took a stern stance. "How the hell can you do all of that? I have been here five years and seen three other plant managers come and go. You've been here for a month and haven't done anything."

I stood my ground and said, "If I can get a commitment from all of you guys to trust me for six months, we can turn this place around. I have a four-point plan that will help us. I absolutely cannot do it without support, though. I don't know the process well enough. You all and the front-line team know the operation. There are things we have to improve, but I have spent at least a little time with everyone. We have good people here with decent attitudes. We have smart managers here who just need the right focus. We are spread too thin working on the wrong goals. Look, this economy is tough and I'm offering you a chance. The worst thing that will happen is that I am wrong and we will all lose our jobs anyways."

My leg was literally shaking and I was praying that no one noticed it for fear that it would influence their decision. I just needed someone, just one person, to back me up out of the nine. If one person was remotely positive then I had a gut feeling that the lemming effect would take over the rest of them. I waited. No one spoke out loud. I did hear Henry whisper something in Scott's ear, but I couldn't discern what was said. I waited some more; it had been about three minutes. There was no way I could do this by myself.

Finally, after what seemed like an eternity, Steve, the logistics manager, spoke up. "Alright, I will give you six months of my all. So what is your plan?"

I found out at next year's holiday party that Steve went to West Point. Being a former army officer, he just wanted to lead and be led. As expected, I got a few more very supportive agreements and a few insincere ones.

"Ok," I said. "Let's talk about the plan!"

The Plan

I put up the first slide for the team:

Our Plan for World-Class Manufacturing

❑ Safety is the number one priority

I definitely saw the whites of the team's eyes get a bit bigger.

Sara commented, "We have heard a lot of managers say this before, but it is always just lip service."

"I agree. Over my career, I have dealt with the double talk from managers that say 'safety first' in front of the main team, but in the back room they are screaming at the line managers for more revenue. This is a fundamental concept that we must embrace right now."

Sara inquired, "What metrics are we going to have for safety? We have to stop having injuries. We had three injuries last year; if we don't fix this problem, we will end up losing our jobs."

I thought about what she said for a few seconds. "That is probably a true statement. The problem with the injuries measurement is that we can't do anything about it once it has already happened. Also, if I tell you to be careful, what action can you really take? We need to focus on things that we can control. We need actionable steps for our team. If we had three injuries in the last twelve months, then you can bet that a lot more is going on out there than that. We have to engage our team to tell us their problems instead of covering them."

Safety Improvement Concepts

- ❑ Never discipline someone for identifying a problem
- ❑ Create a system to expose safety deficiencies & opportunities
- ❑ Empower the team to feel comfortable to shut down operations for a safety concern

Scott interrupted me. "What you are asking is an impossible task! The guy you replaced would discipline the team for bringing problems to light. He even terminated a guy for getting hurt. The company got sued; it was really bad."

I nodded my head. "That makes a lot of sense. During my gemba walks I have noticed uneasiness among the front-line team. We are in a hole, but the first thing we have to do is stop digging. Once one of our team feels empowered by us setting the example, the others will follow suit."

Kellen, who had been quiet for a good while, finally chimed in, "What in the world is a 'gemba walk'?"

"Gemba is Japanese for 'the real place.' We all need to spend more time on the floor so we can know, not *think* we know, what is going on out there."

I issued the following edict to the team:

No one is allowed to use his or her computer before 9:00 am or after 3:00 pm.

Based on the reaction, a bystander would have thought I had kidnapped their children.

Sara started crying. "There is no way I can get all of these safety and environmental procedures, work instructions and requirements completed with six hours less of computer time each day."

Sara had just given herself away that she had been working twelve hours a day. The only question was for how long had this been occurring. Johnny passed Sara a tissue; I was starting to see that the six-foot-four grizzly bear was really a big teddy bear.

"Sara, my perception is that you have been doing this work instruction updates and other data mining for a long time and we are still getting people hurt. Is that correct?"

She had finally composed herself and said, "Yes, but I have to do it or the corporate safety director will fire me. She's going to probably have me fired either way."

Leadership Learnings: When you are stuck in a double-bind situation you are going to disappoint someone. That is, sometimes, the price of being a leader.

"So if you are going to be fired either way, what does it matter what you try to do? Would you rather be typing away at the computer for eleven or twelve hours each day or would you rather keep your team safe? To my knowledge, there are no legal requirements for you to have these procedures. Sara, I am now your direct supervisor and I will take this monkey off of your back."

I took a short pause and continued. "We will engage our team and get safety improvement ideas and praise near-miss reporting. Don't worry too much about the details at this point. We will get in motion first and then fill in the gaps."

I clicked up my second slide.

Our Plan for World-Class Manufacturing

- ❑ Safety is the number one priority
- ❑ Increase unit throughput 20%

"Second goal: We will increase throughput by 20%."

This time I think George wanted to cry. "How in the world are we supposed to get 20% more product out the door in one year? And where is your productivity target - is that next?"

"I'm not interested in productivity improvements. I think we will hit 50% throughput improvement in one year, but I didn't want to scare you all."

George thundered in, "On our best year ever, we had a 4% productivity improvement and I think we were up 2% from a throughput perspective."

I was doing everything I could not to seem arrogant when I said, "George, productivity is meaningless. Our core business at this site is to sell resin. We don't make more money by cutting heads to increase a number on paper. We have to do the right thing for our team, secure their jobs, and even hire more people when the time is right. If we increase our throughput by 20%, then our productivity number will go up by default."

Lean Learnings: You cannot save your way to profitability. Frugality has its place: we do not want to waste money, but cutting cost should not be the first knob the management wants to turn.

"The bottom line is that we want to create a culture that exposes problems instead of hiding them. Traditional manufacturing hides problems for short term results. Lean manufacturing puts it in the spotlight so we can have a team take ownership of them and solve them."

Kellen spoke up in a half excited tone. "I heard about that in the training I went to at the operations management conference. It seemed too simple to work. Have you ever seen this done before?"

"Kellen, I'm not going to lie to you: we did this at my last site, but the spirit wasn't right. It's what I call check-the-box improvement. The management didn't genuinely care about the people. We were able to get some improvements, but it wasn't the same as a Toyota factory."

I continued in a more upbeat fashion. "We can change that, though. I had the opportunity to study under a retired executive who was a master of this. He told me that the spirit of the system was grounded by a genuine love for your team, coupled with systematic process improvement. We need to start running projects and spending money on improvements."

Lean Learnings: The purchasing function tends to become a slow-down point. Do whatever you can to break down this barrier!

George was now in a fit of laughter. "You do realize that Devon is going to kill you. I have been de facto running this place for about four months and I get at least five emails per month telling me to control our spending. What do you want to spend money on? I don't exactly get it."

"I'm glad you asked! We are going to have at least four kaizen events in the next twelve months."

Henry spoke up for the first time. "A kai-what event?"

"A kaizen event. A kaizen event is a week-long improvement event that focuses on exposing the problems with one process, finding out what caused them, and implementing countermeasures. 'Kai' means change in Japanese and 'zen' means good. The literal translation is something like 'a little bit of change for the good.'"

I seemed to get more buy-in out of that last facet of the plan or maybe they were just out of objections. I had a feeling that the last point would revitalize their initial fervor. I showed the third slide.

Our Plan for World-Class Manufacturing

- ❑ Safety is the number one priority
- ❑ Increase unit throughput 20%
- ❑ Analyze demonstrated lead time & cut by 50%; switch to pull system

I decided to take any objections head on. "This goal is really a no-brainer; our kaizen events and throughput improvement will take care of our lead time. The key is switching to a pull system."

Production Scheduling 101

Push System	**Pull System**
Basic Principle: Schedule work based on demand	Basic Principle: Authorize work based on system signals
Best Application	
Stable demand that is easily forecasted	Dynamic response to changing customer demands; unstable demand products
Real Life Examples	
Oil-refinery: Gasoline demand is very stable; production is run to a very steady schedule modeled by economists and software	Supermarket: When the cashier rings up a can of corn on the register, a signal is sent that the can of corn needs to be restocked on the shelves

I expected someone in the logistics department to be up in arms based on George's reaction to the lack of a productivity target. Steve and Tom gave each other the eye and finally Tom stated, "That all sounds great. Both of us are tired of so many customer complaints about late shipments and having to deal with so many back orders. We fight a constant battle between the customer and our customer service department."

"That's understandable," I replied. "Decisions were made to poorly affect your capacity. Additionally, after looking through your warehouse, I see that a lot of the product you do have on shelf is covered in a quarter-inch of dust."

Sara looked to be feeling better about our plan and chimed in, "That's because we were directed by Devon to not ship waste; apparently he wants to make our waste numbers look good so we aren't allowed to ship those expired products."

I segued into my culminating stump speech. I was either going to get a preliminarily engaged team or I was going to be on the internet tonight posting my resume and looking for another endeavor.

"Team, I believe with every fiber of my being that we can help this plant become a world-class manufacturing organization. I can't do it alone. This site is too big. I need some people to dive deep and help."

I was beginning to realize that, in practice, Steve was the leader of the group. He spoke up, looking directly at me. "Look, we all want to keep our jobs; the economy is terrible right now. I like not having to commute fifty or sixty miles from work like I used to. I can safely say that all of us would like this place to shine, but it seems like a far cry from where we are now. Most of us aren't prepared for the 'lean journey' you are talking about. The old plant manager and I went to kaizen leader training a few years ago, but Devon wouldn't let us do it."

I took a deep breath. This was probably the most exhausting meeting I had ever been at. It certainly reminded me why I did not pursue a career in sales. Handling objections day-in, day-out was certainly not my forte.

"Steve, the future of the business at this location is at stake; there are over a hundred jobs here. All of these people have families. I am of the mindset that we should beg for forgiveness and not ask for permission. I will take the heat if something goes horribly awry; I promise."

Leadership Learnings: "You can be rogue, but you have to be right!"

Steve looked a little bit calmer at this point. "We are all very frustrated since Devon took over. I'm not going to say that silly definition of insanity quote. What is our action plan?"

I threw up another slide. "I'm glad that you asked that."

Action Items to Rollout the Plan

- ❑ Communicate truncated message to the team
- ❑ Ubiquitous training
- ❑ Go to the gemba daily- no computer use before 9:00am and after 3:00pm

"Firstly, we will have a first and second shift meeting tomorrow at shift change. We will also sit down with third shift as they come in at 10:00 tomorrow night. George and Steve, I would appreciate it if you would come in then for a few minutes so they can see familiar faces."

They nodded in agreement.

"Next we will start to train like we have never trained before. We will have kaizen leader training for the leadership team; Steve, I can use your help with that. We will do kaizen awareness training for the whole site. We will also get a flat screen monitor for the break room to use 'training by osmosis' for the front-line. It can be very effective. We will keep training until this all becomes natural for us. Concurrent with the training, we all have to get on the floor as much as possible. The gemba must become our natural environment. We are going to discover problems and we must not be alarmed; they are good things. We need the opportunities to feed our list of potential kaizens."

"Do you think the team is really going to give us this large list of potential opportunities? What do we do if they don't?" Kellen asked.

"We just have to create an environment where they will be given the opportunity to be successful and I have to believe that they will meet our expectations."

Kellen still looked concerned but he nodded in agreement.

"Is everybody good to go on the immediate plan? We are having a plant wide meeting tomorrow at 2:00 pm and third shift debrief at 10:00 pm."

Johnny, who had been quiet for a good bit of time, asked, "How will we know when we are ready to have a kaizen?"

I retorted, "When the time is right, we will just know!"

8. DELIVERING THE PLAN & ANOTHER CALL

I don't think I had ever been more anxious than I was driving through the gate to the plant the morning of the plan rollout to the front-line team. I stopped my car to say hi to Marcos. He had become my security blanket of sorts; he was the constant in a sea of variability.

"Good morning, Marcos."

As usual he smiled, but curiously he asked, "Do you think they are going to close the plant down? We have been hearing a lot of rumors."

"Not if I have my say."

"Other managers have said the same thing, but they have come and gone. It is only a matter of time, I think."

"There is a strong team in the plant; they just need to understand that they have the power to make this site world-class. We don't need money or fancy engineers; guys like Dave, running the reactors, and Enrique, the quality control tech, are the heart of this organization. We have to unlock their hidden talents."

"I hope you are right. I've been standing at this gate for six years and I would like to keep it that way."

We shared a final smile and I drove up to the plant. I looked down at my phone and the time showed 5:45 am. I knew that I wasn't going home until about 10:30 tonight. Getting committed didn't bother me, per se; however, I had to put myself in the proper frame of mind. This wasn't going to be a forty-yard dash: it would take many months of driving, supporting, training, failing, adjusting, hoping, and praying. If I were able to take a break by next December, I would have chalked it up in the win column.

I spent the next few hours putting some slides together to get me through the first meeting with some semblance of flow. Suddenly, my cell started vibrating. It bounced off of my desk and landed on the floor next to me. The words plastered across the four inch LCD screen said, "Devon." I picked up the phone and he sounded somewhat pleasant. I didn't dislike him as a person; it was just that our management styles were quite polar.

"I just wanted to let you know that I have a layover near your plant. I will be stopping by tomorrow at around noon for a quick site visit and plant tour."

"That sounds good. Is there anything in particular that you need me to prepare?"

"No, I would like to start with a walk-about and then spend some time with you and the management team."

"Ok, we will see you tomorrow then."

I decided to take a break from my slides for a bit. For the first time since I left my previous job, I felt that empty hole inside of my stomach. I knew that I could get through this, but I didn't know at what cost. I didn't want to be in another situation where I dreaded coming in to work. I decided to call the production manager and logistics manager up to my office so we could strategize the visit with our vice president.

After I told George and Steve what was going on, I got some mixed reactions.

"He never does anything impromptu," said George. "He is coming down here with an agenda."

Steve was a little more even-keeled and replied, "I think this is just a checkup visit on the new plant manager. I wouldn't get scared until he asks to meet with us one-on-one."

"He did say that he wanted to meet with the management team as a group, so that's a positive. How should we play it during the tour?"

George responded, "We just need to make sure that he doesn't wander. I will have the guys clean up tonight."

"No, we don't want to do that. The guys see through that kind of stuff. We want to expose problems, not hide them."

"But we have always done that. He's going to freak out."

"I will deal with those repercussions."

"You are either the smartest guy ever or the dumbest one…I haven't figured it out yet." George sighed.

Steve chimed in, "We are either going to win big or go belly up!"

"Oh, I definitely agree! To me the fear of regret is way worse than failure. I would rather be able to say that I gave it my all than keep us on a failure path."

We shared a last laugh and went back to business until the 2:00 pm meeting.

The Meeting

The time had arrived to advise the team of the new plan. I was still quite a bit anxious, but the camaraderie with Steve and George helped. Little did I know, but those two would become pivotal to the success of the business.

"Good afternoon team! Most of you guys have met me, but some of you haven't. How is everyone doing?"

I got a few murmurings, but nothing significant.

"The reason we are having this meeting is because our business needs to significantly improve or we risk being consolidated into another site or worse yet, the product line altogether could be dropped."

The room got suddenly quiet.

I put up my first slide.

The front-line team had the same expression that the management team had yesterday.

A 26-year employee, Clarence, gave the first outburst. "If we aren't satisfying our customers now, how is slowing down going to help us? We all want to keep our jobs; we need to work faster."

"Working faster is not going to help you satisfy customers, because that isn't a process. Also, quality errors will go up when people take shortcuts. I'd rather send someone no resin than bad resin that messes up his or her machines. Safety and productivity are not mutually exclusive; in fact, they are married. Every time you all have to clean up a machine that is messy or someone leaves a cart in a walkway it costs you time. Accidents cost time. Making this plant safe will help us be more productive. I need everyone in this room to be my eyes and ears. If something leaks, we need to fix it. If a machine isn't running right, submit a work order. Sara is going to work on implementing a safety suggestion card program for me. This will be a direct line of communication to me."

I didn't really appease him, but he didn't ask another question.

I put up the second slide onto the flat screen.

Plant Turnaround Plan

- ❑ Safety is absolutely the first priority
  - ❑ Everyone has the authority to stop unsafe work
  - ❑ The management can't fix problems they don't know about
  - ❑ The team on the floor keeps us safe
- ❑ Kaizen
  - ❑ 3-10 day rapid improvement events
  - ❑ 6-10 person, cross functional teams from all plant personnel

The anticipated response was received.

A relatively new operator, Mark, shouted, "What the heck is a kaizen? I don't speak Japanese!"

"It's actually two words. Kai means change and Zen means good. Literally it means 'change for the good.' I need your help to change this plant for the better. I don't know it inside and out like you all do. This plant is almost thirty years old. There is probably five hundred years of local plant experience in this room. I need a select few of you to be on a team to rethink the way we do business. I need your help."

A fairly seasoned and outspoken operator, Stacy, said, "So what will you be doing?"

The room chuckled and I smiled. I thought I even caught George with a smirk.

"Stacy, that's an excellent question. We are going to teach you all how to see. We will get you all the tools you need to make your personal workspace better. If all of your jobs are not easier by this time next year, I have failed. You should all be doing things less physically and more mentally. It's a cliché, but we have to work smart. If US manufacturing doesn't get smart, all of our jobs will go to India or China. We can win, though, because it takes three months to get product over to the US by boat.

"My two minute overview of a kaizen event goes like this:

1. We take a picture of the process - we map out what is actually happening on the floor.
2. We identify waste in the process.
3. We put ideas in place that stop the waste.
4. We take a picture of the new process and communicate the change.
5. Then we celebrate!

"That is it guys, that's all there is to it. We can either turn this place around and keep our jobs or just stagnate and throw in the towel."

There are a few moments in your life where you think, "I am so glad I did ________." They may occur with something small like remembering to turn off the stove before a trip overseas. My moment was spending many hours on the floor with Dave, the reactor operator. I didn't know exactly what happened, but Dave is a talker. He had told about twenty to thirty of his friends that he had been respected for the first time since he was in high school playing football. Some of those friends told their friends. This communication had wiped away preconceived notions of what I was going to be like. That is exactly what you want during a lean transformation; you want a blank slate ready for knowledge.

Dave spoke up. "Say we do trust you, what do we do next? None of us have ever done a kaizen."

For the first time of my life I felt like I was in a cheesy 1970s martial arts movie. "It's time for your training; we must train until spotting waste is as natural as breathing!"

I answered some more specific questions about the process and proceeded back to my office.

I returned at 10:00 pm to a smaller crowd. Much to my surprise, George, Steve, Johnny, and Sara showed up.

Sara whispered to me, "I hope you really care about safety as much as you say. I've always been treated like an administrator and nothing more."

"We are going to change all that. I promise!"

The meeting went similarly to the first meeting. Apparently the first shift had called the third shift and filled them in before they got here.

I went to the white board and wrote the following and posted a sign-up sheet before I left for the evening:

1. Kaizen Training-
    a. 1st Shift/3rd Shift 6:15 today
    b. 2nd Shift 6:00 pm today
2. Kaizen Leader Training- Sign on the sheet below

As I was walking back to my office, I noticed several associates going to the board and I saw someone googling "kaizen" on their smartphone.

I think we made an impact.

9. MEETING TIM WOOD

I walked into the conference room about 6:00 am and I dropped three boxes of assorted doughnuts on the table. While I was setting up the projector and waiting for the team to arrive, one of my team from the warehouse came in and sat down.

"Hi Glenn. What can I do for you?"

"I was just wondering what made you take this job. Didn't you know we were having problems?"

"Well, most plants have problems. There are very few plants that run the way a Toyota factory does."

"What's so special about the way Toyota runs their factories?"

"It is the way their people interact with each other and the way they see their jobs. Toyota gets upwards of 100,000 employee suggestions for process improvements each and every year."

"Wow. What would you guys do with all of those suggestions?"

"We would give someone a full time job deciding which ones are the best to implement."

Glenn grabbed a doughnut and sat down as the other team members started to take their seats. We had a packed house. Johnny, my first shift production supervisor, took a seat surprisingly close to the front. The box of doughnuts looked like it had been shredded by a pack of rabid wolverines; one thing that is constant in manufacturing facilities is that operators can eat twenty four hours a day, seven days a week.

I turned to my team and boldly stated, "I've been here almost two months now. I have met a lot of good people, but there is one of us who I can't stand. We have to get rid of Tim immediately! He is making all of your jobs more difficult than they have to be; plus, he backs up our docks, clogs the production area with rework, and is one of the main reasons people get hurt here."

At this point the team looked confused, as expected; we had no real person named Tim on site (this works more effectively if you have a Timothy in the room, but you can't win them all!).

I flashed up my first slide.

TIM WOOD Must Leave our Plant

- ❑ Tim Wood is present all around us
- ❑ He makes our jobs more difficult than they should be
- ❑ He costs our plant millions of dollars
- ❑ Tim Wood is waste
- ❑ He must be eliminated

Johnny was starting to get a little frustrated. "Ok we get it - there is something you don't like about the plant."

I tried to play a little coy and said, "Johnny, you hate him worse than I do. You will do everything you can to get rid of him, because as a first-line supervisor, he causes 90% of your problems. Your team is numb to him; however, he is crushing you."

I paused for a few moments and said, "I'll get to the point. Tim Wood is an acronym for waste. Tim Wood is all the types of waste that occur in the plant, office, hospital, wherever."

The team looked relieved after I explained myself. I needed to do this to grab their attention.

I transitioned to my second slide.

TIM WOOD is Waste

- ❑ T = Transportation waste

"Ok team, does anyone have any idea what transportation waste is?"

Mark spoke up and said, "I dunno, moving something when you don't really have to do it."

I retorted quickly, "Absolutely! That's perfect. Where do we have transportation waste in the plant?"

Mark spoke again. "Nowhere; everything I do is for a reason. I have to package out product."

Johnny chimed in, "Are you kidding me? When we package resin into five gallon pails as base for the consumer industry, how many pallets do you have to move to find those pails?"

"Mark, do me a favor," I said. "Go out to the plant and find out how many pallets you have to move to get the five gallon pails out of stock."

Mark eagerly threw his safety glasses and hard hat back on and scurried out the conference room door.

"Ok team, let's look at waste number two."

TIM WOOD is Waste

- ❑ T = Transportation waste
- ❑ I = Inventory waste

"Who knows what inventory waste is?"

"Having a surplus of raw materials or finished goods," Steve offered.

"Great. Carrying any more inventory than is necessary to supply customer requirements is waste. Failed batches are another type of waste that creates inventory waste. Who here likes reworking a batch? I sure didn't. Dave had a big grin on his face while I was adding rework to the reactor small addition station."

At exactly the right time, Mark came storming back into the room; he paused to catch his breath and shouted, "Twenty three! I have to move twenty three pallets because the five gallon pails are buried."

"Wow, that's some serious transportation waste. I bet it takes about an hour or so to just get them."

"Yes, it does and the product becomes harder to package as it cools down. Usually my first batch of the five gallons takes three times as long as the drums or bulk containers."

"And I bet it's frustrating having to move all those pallets?"

"It's horrible," Mark said. "It's like getting on an elevator where someone's kid has pushed all the buttons and you are on the twenty-fifth floor going to one!"

"That's a great analogy! Mark, do you hate Tim Wood?"

"I do now! He's been making my life hard for a long time and I didn't even know it!"

I flashed up my next slide.

TIM WOOD is Waste

- ❑ T = Transportation waste
- ❑ I = Inventory waste
- ❑ M = Motion waste

"Anyone want to take a guess?"

By this point in time, I had most of the class engaged. A few of the third shifters were drifting, but it was to be expected.

"Motion waste," I said, "is similar to the transportation waste. Transportation waste is associated with moving products or materials; motion waste has to do with you, the worker. Anything from looking for tools to do your job, gathering information by looking through catalogs, walking back and forth between operating areas, is a waste. You shouldn't have to walk twenty miles a day to do your job."

In Lee, a middle aged Korean man who had about thirty years of service, chimed in. "I keep telling you guys to clean up your zone. I never have to hunt for my tools, because they are always in the right spot."

I found it interesting that the team was so readily able to point out their faults. I couldn't tell at this point if it was going to be a good thing or not.

"Time for the next waste."

TIM WOOD is Waste

- ❑ T = Transportation waste
- ❑ I = Inventory waste
- ❑ M = Motion waste
- ❑ W = Waiting waste

"This is an easy one. Who can give me an example of waiting waste?"

Johnny spoke up, "Steve, I love you, but once or twice a shift I have guys waiting for material for about an hour. They used to go get it themselves, but you have stressed that they were causing inventory problems."

Steve seemed a little bit irritated, but he took a breath and commented, "Johnny, I understand what you are saying, but if one of my truck loaders or pickers is on vacation or out sick, the material handler has to do two jobs. We still have a staffing problem in the warehouse."

I quickly interjected, "Johnny, that's a good example of waste; at this point we just want to identify. The good thing about kaizen is that there is no blame. Steve doesn't intentionally do this to production. Does that make sense - we all want to help each other?"

I got a bunch of nods throughout the room. I was secretly very happy that there was confrontation between two of my managers. Interactions like that will help them grow if there is a facilitator to prevent it from spiraling into an emotional issue.

"Time for the first 'O'."

TIM WOOD is Waste

- ❑ T = Transportation waste
- ❑ I = Inventory waste
- ❑ M = Motion waste
- ❑ W = Waiting waste
- ❑ O = Overproduction waste

"Hmm, overproduction waste. Does anyone have an idea?"

Nick, the first shift lead operator, asked, "Is it making something we don't need? We have old product sitting in the racks that no one wants; yet it pops up on the schedule from time to time."

"The corporate inventory group has me make this stuff. I have told them a dozen times it's not moving, but apparently the sales team wants it ready for when they close the sale," Johnny replied.

I asked curiously, "Why not just make it when an order comes in?"

"I asked that very question, but apparently the customers we don't have yet will want it shipped out the next day," he replied sarcastically.

I went over to my email and drafted a quick note. I said, "I can take care of that one easily. You all have to let me know about this stuff, though, or I can't fix it.

"Very good, we are almost through Mr. Wood. Waste number six."

TIM WOOD is Waste
❑ T = Transportation waste
❑ I = Inventory waste
❑ M = Motion waste
❑ W = Waiting waste
❑ O = Overproduction waste
❑ O = Overprocessing waste

"This is probably the toughest one to understand. Does anyone want to give it a shot?"

I didn't get any responses; a couple of the team members had their hands about a third of the way up, but they put them back down.

"Ok, no problem. Over processing waste would be like taking one of those fifty five gallon drums and gift wrapping it before sending it to the next chemical plant. The chemical plant doesn't care about a requirement to have gift wrap on a raw material drum. Did that help anyone think of another example?"

Dave stood up. "You know for about three years now I have heard the drivers for one of our smaller accounts saying that the company would buy twice as much from us if we would sell them our rejected material and they would blend it into our good material. They don't need to have our tight specs for their process."

"Excellent, we need to look into that deeper. You made a very good point. The bottom line is we need to ask our customers what *they* want, not deliver what we *think* they want. Very good Dave!

"All right, it's time for my most hated waste. This one has us literally dropping money on the floor and spitting all over it."

TIM WOOD is Waste
❑ T = Transportation waste
❑ I = Inventory waste
❑ M = Motion waste
❑ W = Waiting waste
❑ O = Overproduction waste
❑ O = Overprocessing waste
❑ D = Defect waste

"George, what is our defect rate for resin? What percentage of prime material do we make?"

George thought about it for a minute and replied, "About eighty to ninety percent, I think."

Enrique, one of our quality control technicians said, "Last month we had 81.4% prime off the line."

"Very good," I said. "That's a huge waste. Who here in the department would like to do half as much rework processing?"

Literally a sea of hands bounced up in the air.

"It is easy. All we have to do is get that number up to over ninety percent every month and we will be there! That will eliminate other wastes as well. Less inventory waste, less transportation waste, less motion waste."

George sighed and asked, "So what number do you want us to get to? This wasn't in your original plan."

"Don't worry about the number; we just want to get better. The main goal is to create that environment where we expose the problems and then solve them. A number on a piece of paper isn't going to give me a warm-fuzzy. Does that make sense?'"

George snorted and laughed, "No, but I like your answer."

I turned off the projector and asked if there were any questions.

"When can we start firing Tim Wood?" asked Johnny, half-jokingly.

"We need more training first; this isn't something we want to rush into. All in due time."

Johnny smiled and like clockwork my phone rang. I answered and it was Devon.

"Good morning! I got in early and I will be at the plant in about forty five minutes."

"All right, I will see you soon!"

The high feeling I got from talking about the seven wastes quickly dissipated into a nervous energy. I hated being in a situation like this. I was going against the grain on almost everything he told me, but I knew it was for the good of the business.

10. THE GEMBA WALK

Several years ago I had the opportunity to learn from a consulting group that was composed of retired Toyota team members. Although I consider the time life-altering, I can only recall two things that the senior consultant told me (through an interpreter):

1. Don't brainstorm; try-storm. The difference between lean engineers and non-lean engineers comes in the planning stage. Non-lean engineers prefer to spend a large amount of time on the design board considering every possible scenario. Lean engineers make a prototype and all the scenarios that are applicable will reveal themselves during testing.

2. Go out onto the shop floor and see what is really taking place. You cannot manage from the office; you must position yourself on the floor where the value is created to make proper decisions about improving the process.

This formula seemed all too simple; perhaps the simplicity of it was what made it hard to understand. You don't need a PhD in engineering or psychology to go out on the floor and engage the front-line team. This thought played over and over again in my head and then, as if out of nowhere, a black town car drove through the gate and parked in front of the building.

Marcos had given me a heads up that Devon had arrived, but even with the preparation, the feelings of anticipation had overtaken me. This was my first time running my own site; it was the equivalent of giving a sixteen-year old the keys to dad's new Porsche. The feelings of self-doubt had to be pushed out of my head so I could attend to my visitor.

Devon was signing the visitor log when I walked down to the lobby to meet him.

"Good afternoon," I said jovially.

"Hello there," he replied.

I buzzed him into the front door and escorted him down to the spare office next to mine.

"How much time do you need?"

He responded, "Give me about fifteen minutes and I will be ready."

"Ok, I will get the team together and we will do a plant walk."

I gave Steve and George a call so that both of them could be present during the plant tour. I would need the extra sets of eyes and their process knowledge to keep me stable during this visit. It was very possible that Devon could ask me a question that I did not know the answer to. I did not know if this was the case with respect to Devon, but in traditional mass production the site managers were supposed to be the oracles and not being able to answer his questions would be a chink in my proverbial suit of armor. Contrast this with the consulting group that I had worked with who took the Socratic approach: "When you know you know nothing, you will be prepared."

Devon was finishing up a short conference call when Steve and George made their way up to my office.

George asked, "So how do you think this is going to go?"

"I was hoping you two would tell me that!" I replied.

Steve turned out to be the calm one. "It's going to be fine; he doesn't know that we are changing the game plan."

"I hope you are right. I know that the methods will work for us; we just have to bear some fruit. Once we prove to the organization as a whole that we are superstars, it will be easy."

George inquisitively asked, "What if you are wrong? What if we run five kaizens and get nothing? What then? It is nice to see your confidence, but what if we fail?"

I had honestly not considered it from that perspective. To me, running kaizens and capitalizing on the front-line team's knowledge just made sense. I had self-doubt that existed internally, but the process was foolproof. Other companies had done it before.

After an extra fifteen minutes and more discussion between the three of us, Devon exited the office. George started with a quick safety brief and then we made our way out into the plant.

We first passed through the packaging area of the plant. It was a bit strange; normally I would see a lot of hustle and today the place looked like a ghost town. I saw a front-line associate bolt off in the other direction after catching a glimpse of our tour group. This was not good.

We finally saw a packaging operator setting up the machine for a new product type. Nick was adept at setting up his machines and he took a certain level of pride in it.

"Where is your set up procedure?" Devon asked very directly.

Nick replied nervously, "Um… I think it is in the binder over there near the super's office."

Nick motioned over to the supervisor's office as if he was about to start walking in that direction, but I stopped him. I went and fetched the dusty book from the rack and opened it up. The book was obviously outdated and did not include the necessary information. The pages had begun to yellow from age. No one had looked at this book in quite some time. I wouldn't have either. It was set up like stereo instructions: no one could reasonably understand what was going on. From my perspective, Nick had done no wrong, but I didn't know how Devon would take it so I preemptively struck.

"George, would you mind making a note of this? We need better standard work instructions for the operations team. We can't expect them to follow antiquated work instructions such as these. I will send you some templates for creating visual work instructions. Make sure you have Nick or another packaging operator helping you create them. We have to get their knowledge on paper before we lose it."

Devon looked like he was about to say something, but did not. He seemed slightly confused by my retort, but there was no way to tell what he was thinking.

We made our way to bulk raw material storage and Devon made some comments regarding a ladder that was supposed to have some additional guarding and some labeling that was missing. I gave George a nod and he took some pictures with his phone. We continued to the reaction area of the plant.

Dave was in the reaction area of the plant doing his traditional happy-go-lucky routine. There even seemed to be some extra bounce in his step. As soon as he saw the group walk into the room, he came over immediately.

"I made a list of some of the wastes that we have coming out of the reaction area."

He handed me a slip of paper.

Reaction Area Waste

- ❑ T = Transportation waste
  - ❑ Broken bulk transfer
- ❑ I = Inventory waste
  - ❑ Unused raw materials for months
  - ❑ Unshipped product
- ❑ M = Motion waste
  - ❑ Walking to find tools
  - ❑ Walking up and down ladder to load reactor
  - ❑ Loading rework
- ❑ W = Waiting waste
  - ❑ Waiting for raw materials from warehouse
  - ❑ Waiting to pump out reactor
- ❑ O = Overproduction waste
  - ❑ Producing wrong product
- ❑ D = Defect waste
  - ❑ Failed batches

"Very good Dave!" I exclaimed.

George's mouth literally dropped in awe.

Dave responded, "That's just what I have been working on since we had training. I know that there is a lot more going on out here. Didn't you tell me that most processes have a significant portion of waste?"

"Yes," I said. "Most processes are 90% waste. We have to find the right opportunities to focus on. Make sure that you guys keep looking at your processes for waste."

"George, do you mind if we create some way to log our ideas?" Dave asked.

George looked a bit puzzled, as if no one had asked him a question like that before. "Why don't you get a new white board out of the supply room and post your observations. If I know this team, a competition will start and we will soon have ten posted sheets."

"Excellent!" I replied. "At this point we want to make sure we are focusing on identification only. Kaizen events are the time for us to develop solutions. Not that we can't improve things throughout the year, but we want multiple team members putting their heads together for an optimal solution."

Devon rapidly scratched some notes in his book and asked Dave for another copy of the paper. Dave went to his workstation and produced a copy for Devon.

The rest of the plant tour was basically uneventful. Devon was pushing to get back to the conference room so we could sit and talk. George and Steve would later tell me that these tours were usually much more painful than this. George even went as far as to say that they occasionally lingered six hours or more.

The four of us sat back down in the conference room. I was curious as to how this would unfold. George's expressions, which had now become my barometer for how well the day was going, had finally started to relax. All things considered, I felt things could have gone a lot worse.

Devon scratched some additional notes before speaking. "So what are your plans to improve productivity in the reaction area?"

Out of nowhere, like a bolt of lightning, George responded, "We are going to run a week-long kaizen event on the reaction area."

Devon gave George a blank stare as if he was saying, "you better tell me whats going on and quickly.".

Steve continued, "We are going to have a cross-functional team attack that problem specifically. We will take members from all functions at our plant and put them together for a week to attack production in that unit. We will develop a list of countermeasures for stifled productivity and then strategically eliminate them."

Devon made some additional notes in his book. I know that he asked some additional questions that day, but I cannot for the life of me remember what they were. About forty five minutes later he excused himself to make the trip back to the airport. We all shook hands; then he departed. The last thing I remember him telling me was that he would be in touch next week.

After the meeting I went to Steve and George, excited. "Wow guys! I didn't realize that you two were genuinely excited about running a kaizen."

George quipped, "We aren't. I am scared to death of that guy. He seemed softer today. I just don't think you understand what he's done to the organization. I also don't think you know how hard it is going to be to get the other operators on board like Dave."

Steve nodded and communicated the same concerns to me.

He also said, "I'm having problems getting product out the door now. I don't know if I will be able to facilitate a whole week with reduced shipping staff."

I'm usually the type of person that wants to handle objections such as these. I wanted to say, "Guys, that's why we need kaizen. It's not a reason to stop it." However, I decided to hold my tongue. I needed someone else in the organization with some belief in this.

Steve and George went back to their offices. I answered a few emails and set up my next day's to-do list. My cell phone suddenly rang. I was half expecting it to be Devon, but it flashed with Johnny's name.

"Hey Johnny, what can I do for you?"

"I just wanted to give you some data quickly. We have about an hour and a half worth of downtime every shift on the main reactor waiting for the warehouse to bring us raw materials. That's a huge amount of waste. Is there any way we can work on that now? I don't think we should wait months for the first kaizen event."

"Yes Johnny, we absolutely can fix it. Bring two front-line associates to my office tomorrow morning and snag George on your way up."

11. THE FIRST LEAN TOOL

I was driving up to the gate the next morning and Marcos waved as I approached.

"I see that you survived and came back to us! Sometimes after he comes down we lose a manager for a couple of months and then someone new drives up and introduces themself to me."

"You aren't going to get rid of me that easily; hopefully I will be seeing your smiling face for the next couple of years."

I walked down the hallway to my office. I had planned on settling my belongings and preparing for my meeting with Johnny and the team. Much to my surprise, Johnny was down in the conference room with the projector warming up and three of the white boards full of information. I can't tell you how much time he had spent preparing for this meeting, but it was obvious he wanted to remove Tim Wood from this part of the operation.

A few minutes later we were positioned in the conference room with Johnny at the front, ready to make a small presentation. The following team members were in attendance:

Johnny - Production Supervisor, Resin Reaction
George - Production Manager
Dave - Resin Reaction Operator
Nick - Resin Packaging Operator

Johnny seemed a bit nervous. I don't think that he had given that many (or any) presentations like these recently. I take for granted that I am talking in front of others a significant portion of my day.

"Ok team, I got the plant manager's permission yesterday to pull you guys together and solve the problem of waiting for material. As you know,

Dave, I have had the lead reaction operator take a log for the last several days about downtime associated with waiting for raw materials. It turned out to be significant." Johnny flashed up *his* first slide.

"These delays were captured over the last several days and they are leading to direct production reductions. If we can reduce these delays, we will be able to improve the amount of product we can produce and subsequently knock out some of our $2 million dollar backlog."

I looked over these numbers for a few minutes and scribbled some notes in my book.

"Johnny, are there any other problems associated with the current process other than the waiting waste?"

Johnny passed out a chart of some data he had been gathering.

Raw Material Delay Time (Total Minutes)

	Day 1	Day 2	Day 3	Day 4	Day 5	Day 6
1st Shift	40	55	30	40	50	55
2nd Shift	30	50	55	50	60	45
3rd Shift	80	75	85	60	70	85

"I'm glad you asked that. Once or twice per day we have defects associated with the material delivery process. Most of the time this is caught and just reprocessed. Occasionally, it is not caught and ends up in the product. The batch will usually fail, but this is not caught until after the sample is pulled during packaging. At this point it is too late."

Dave spoke up. "We usually don't catch it when it is a wrong raw material from the same manufacturer in the same or similar packaging."

"George, would you agree with this?"

George begrudgingly agreed. It was obvious that Steve and he were friends and he didn't want to throw him under the bus. "Yes, I agree for the most part; obviously, I haven't verified the data."

"These are good observations. What we need to do now is get Steve and a material handler down here so we can get their input and perspective and then implement some countermeasures."

I gave Steve a call on his cell and had him come down to the conference room with an associate who could work in the material handling role.

I wanted to take this from a neutral perspective. I had the feeling that Steve would get a bit defensive when the numbers were shown on the screen. It was obvious he took pride in his work and I didn't want him to feel attacked. I led the conversation after a few minutes of banter.

"Johnny thinks he has found us an opportunity to bust some waste! If we do it right, we can also make your team's life easier."

Steve looked a bit concerned when he said, "Go ahead. I'm listening."

Johnny flashed up the slide again with the raw material delay and before Steve could react I interjected, "Trevor, would you say these times are reasonable?"

Trevor was a young, single guy who pretty much had a nonchalant outlook on life. The guys thought he worked here just to pay for his sports car. Notwithstanding, he was very smart and always willing to chip in.

"If anything, I would say these times are light. If I'm tied up loading a truck, it could be an hour before I get back to my raw material delivery. Also, this is just with respect to the reaction area. I have many other operators that I have to service," Trevor responded.

"Ok, so we've got this issue identified. How do we solve it?"

In retrospect, I wish I had been able to coach Johnny a little bit before the meeting so that he could have steered the solution. All things considered, we were at a good point. He brought the site an initial opportunity for the application of some lean tools. My mentality was that we needed to have a small victory prior to the first kaizen event to empower the team for success. This would be almost like priming a continuous improvement pump.

"Hmm…let's see. Dave, why don't you walk us through the current process?"

"Um…ok. When I need materials to load my next batch, I call the material handler on the radio and tell him what stuff I need to prepare it."

"How is that working out for you?" I responded.

"Not so good. I usually wait about 5 minutes and then go looking for Trevor or go over to Steve's office."

Everyone chuckled. It was obvious that there was no real process associated with this. We would later find that Steve had set up the material handlers only because the operators kept causing inventory adjustments.

"Ok Dave. Nick, feel free to chime in, too, if you have anything else that Dave is missing from his perspective. So, Dave, when do you know you are going to need the material for the next batch?"

Dave thought about it for a minute. "Is this a trick question? I know what batch I will be making next as soon as I start up the first batch?"

"Ok, that makes sense. How much time elapses between starting up the first batch and loading the second batch?" I knew the answer to this question from my time on the floor, but I find that asking questions is more effective than giving answers when the overall goal is to empower the team.

Dave thought about it. "It depends on the product type, but a minimum of six hours and it could be as much as twenty four," he said.

"So why are we placing an order when we need the material instead of placing it before the material? Is there a problem with delivering it early?"

Dave looked confused. "Why would we want to order it early? I don't have to load it for up to another day."

"That's a good point. Ideally you would want it arriving about a minute before you used it, but realistically that's not going to be feasible."

George looked a bit silly at this point and said, "I generally like to place orders for toiletries before I need them. If we run out of mouth wash or deodorant, it could have serious consequences."

Everyone laughed again and I felt like we were making some headway. Even Steve, who seemed a bit defensive at first, had let his guard down when he realized no one was playing the proverbial blame game.

"Ok, so we figured out that the radio isn't working. It causes quality problems and isn't always staffed. What kind of interface can we use between departments? How can we let logistics know in advance that we need their help?"

George offered a first suggestion to the problem. "What if we sent them an email? Could we set up a dumb terminal to place orders with?"

"That is possible but it is kind of expensive. We would eventually have to add four to five terminals on the floor and one for the material handler," Johnny replied back.

I said, "That's doable, but let's see if we can get something simpler."

Nick, who had previously been quiet, blurted out, "My car broke down a couple of days ago and I tied a white shirt to the antenna. About fifteen minutes later a police car stopped to help me."

"Excellent Nick! Now let's go slightly more high tech than that. Come on. You all are so close."

"We can use an andon light," Steve suggested. "We learned about them vaguely in one of the classes that I took about kaizen events. It has been a while, but it is coming back to me."

"Very good! Andon is the Japanese word for light. Technically it is one of those traditional lanterns that are enshrouded in rice paper. For our purposes it means a signal.

"So the person we need to ask here is Trevor. Trevor, where would be the best place for you to receive a signal? Where are you most apt to see it?"

Trevor got up and moved to the white board and started sketching out the loading docks. He looked at it for a few seconds and then asked, "Can I go out to the floor real quick?"

Johnny quipped, "No, but you can go to the gemba."

Everyone laughed. My eccentricities were fairly obvious and I used a lot of the Japanese words to make a point. To me it was a good thing that I was getting a healthy amount of ribbing. Trevor went out to the floor to get a better look at the loading dock and how he would be responding to the future andon system.

"Ok, so an andon system has several parts:

1. A signal, which is a light.
2. A responder, who is the material handler.
3. An action for the responder to take, which is to bring the raw material order to the operator.

"The previous process was to call out the raw materials over the two-way radio. What can we use in its place? Let's get a quick list of ideas."

Steve spoke up. "We could have the operators write down their order on an order form and attach it near the andon light switch."

"I think we are on the right track, but I'd rather not have them hand write it." Johnny's nervous tone imparted his concern. "We have enough challenges getting the team to write correct lot numbers and consumption amounts on the manufacturing orders."

Dave cautiously asked, "Can we do it the lazy way?"

"Absolutely! The lazier the better. All of these process improvements should make your lives easier. I think I said this before, but if your job isn't easier this time next year, then I have failed!" I acknowledged.

Dave continued, "Why don't we have refrigerator magnets for all of the items that need to be delivered to us? We can post a magnet board and use the magnets to 'write' the order."

"That would certainly eliminate the possibility of transcription errors, Steve answered.

George looked scared at the prospect. "There are at least 200 raw materials between five processes and many of them overlap. That's a whole lot of magnets."

"Team! I think this is a great idea. George is making a valid point. We need to be, what I call, 'ambitiously lazy.' We need to set up systems like this that take some upfront preparation, but solve significant problems once they are up and running. We've been here about two hours now. Johnny, do you have enough information to put a rough idea together and present to us all again tomorrow at eight o'clock? Make sure you pull in Frankie; we are going to have to pull some wire."

"I'm good to go. Steve, do you mind if I pull some of your team to ask them their thoughts? I want to make sure this is operator friendly on your end, too. Unless I'm looking at this wrong, we should never have to interrupt truck loading again!" Johnny was starting to see the possibilities.

Steve smiled. "If you can do that I will kiss you! We have been getting significant detention charges lately. That's literally giving away money!"

We reconvened the next morning and I expected to have more notes or some slides. Much to my surprise, Johnny had built a working prototype on a three-foot by four-foot white board.

Material Handling Andon Board	
Raw Material Order Product Cycle Time:	Production Schedule
	Returns
	Item List <Magnet Storage>

"Wow! You have been busy. Talk to me."

Johnny was nothing less than totally fired up about this idea. I mentioned before that Johnny would be my key lean leader in the organization, but it wasn't until now that I realized how much of a driver he was. It was almost as if something had blown out his pilot light before and we were now beginning to see it glow again.

"George," Johnny said, "there are 160 raw materials associated with the reaction area." Johnny smiled and then continued, "We added a couple of extra sections to the board after talking to the team last night.

1. The team on the third shift wanted a return section. We don't use all of the materials all of the time and it would be nice not to have them piling up on the floor.
2. We will post a cycle time on the board for each product. That will let the material handler know how much of a delay is allowable in case

he cannot deliver immediately. This is important during the last week of the month where volume tends to be higher.

3. We also wanted to post a production schedule to let logistics associates on the floor know what was coming their way so they could call the outside warehouse if necessary.

"We need five of these boards and Trevor has come up with locations for each light by the loading docks. Do you think we can roll this out?"

"Of course. Why wouldn't we?" I responded curiously.

I figured out what had been stifling Johnny without anyone saying a word. He had probably previously had a great deal of ideas and no one would let him drive the change. Frustrated people eventually give up.

"Ok, does anyone have any issues with this process?"

No one spoke up so I gave Johnny the go ahead to run a trial with the first board and then propagate the others.

I sat in my chair at the end of the day watching the sunset from my office and playing back the interactions between the different departments. After about ten minutes, I realized…it's time to move onto kaizen leader training.

12. BACK TO THE CLASSROOM

It had been about three weeks since the prototype material handling board went up. The first process change was met with relatively little resistance. There were a few issues that needed to be tweaked, but no serious showstoppers. One white board and 160 raw material magnets quickly expanded into five whiteboards and over a thousand magnets. The material handlers were the team that was most enthusiastic about the change. The production team was merely waiting for an order while the material handler was being pulled in two or three different directions. This gave them a permissible delay and a way to be able to manage their time more effectively.

Once the prototypes were in full swing, flashing lights began appearing in the warehouse. First one and then another one began slowly morphing the shop floor.

A few of the logistics operators joked, "Thanks for letting us put up lights for the holidays!"

On January second, I put up a note next to the kaizen leader training sign-up that we needed three more volunteers and that the posting would come down in three days.

I ended up with the following team attending kaizen leader training:

Kaizen Leader Training Participants
❑ George - Production Manager ❑ Johnny - Production Supervisor ❑ Henry - Production Supervisor ❑ Steve - Logistics Manager ❑ Frankie - Maintenance Manager ❑ Sara - Health & Safety Specialist ❑ Kellen - Process Engineer ❑ Enrique - QA Tech

As we were about to begin training, I sensed that, overall, the team was anxious. I don't think I will ever know why for sure, but I think the pace of the transformation might have been getting to them. Then there was Johnny; he looked like a ten-year old anxious to open up presents on his birthday. He had two kinds of paper for taking notes --regular and graph-- and even had brought a digital recorder in case he missed something. He got a bit of ribbing from the rest of the team.

George asked, "Johnny, are you moonlighting as a paparazzi?"

Everyone else chuckled and then Johnny said, "I've been totally sold since we started putting those boards in. Steve, I bet you have less truckers that are complaining about detention charges, correct?"

Steve shook his head and said, "Yes, definitely."

I said, "That's the power of creating an operations system that solves problems instead of hiding them!"

"Ok team. We have just been poking at this lean transformation with a stick until now. Running a successful kaizen event is what separates the rubber from the road. It is a very simple process. Complicating it and constraining it with too many rules will hurt our chances for success."

I flashed up my first slide.

Week-long Kaizen Event

- ❑ Take a picture of the process to spot the waste

"The first step in running a kaizen event is to figure out what is going on. However, you can't just simply go on assumptions. You have to get to a minute level of detail to find the waste. It is time for an exercise. Split yourselves up into two teams. We are going to make process flow diagrams for familiar processes."

I changed slides.

Yellow Sticky Process Flow Maps

- ❑Use yellow sticky note to record individual process steps on a white board
- ❑Use succinct format:
  - – Verb + noun if possible
  - – E.g.- Pick 1 bag

Verb + Noun

Time Required | Responsible Party

"Everyone take a pack of yellow stickies and I want you guys to make process flow maps of the following activities:

1. Team 1 - Make a process flow map for preparing a ham and cheese sandwich.
2. Team 2 - Make a process flow map for washing and drying the laundry.

"I'm going to take a quick lap around the plant; I will be back in about fifteen minutes for us to discuss your maps."

As I walked around the plant, I thought about the first kaizen that I was the leader of at my last company. That company had a fake lean system. What I mean is that they didn't have any concern for the well-being of people. In a true lean culture, the front-line associate should be placed on a pedestal. They print the cash for the organization.

I kept wondering if I was going to be able to empower the team to turn this organization around. Having never been in this situation before or even running my own site, the self-doubt was kicking in.

As I returned to the room both teams were seated and ready to go. Both teams had very elaborate process maps constructed that explained virtually every detail.

"Ok, that's great! Now I want you to label the value-added and non-value added activities."

As expected I got a question regarding the two.

"A value-added activity is something you could invoice the customer for. Reacting the resin is value-added. Moving the raw materials from the south end warehouse to the floor is not something you can invoice the customer for and is, therefore, non-value added."

As they were labeling the process flow diagrams I thought back to an incident with my old manager Tony. I had been on site for only about three months.

Tony started screaming, "What is wrong with you? Why did you miss the shipment?"

I answered, "Well, the process is kind of broken; there is an exception on international shipments that…"

"I don't want to hear any more of your excuses. You are never going to get this right."

I remember being so frustrated that I wanted to scream and I did scream when I left that night. I thought back to my talk with Dave; he told me that the previous manager did the same thing to the associates here. It's very easy to tear down a house. It only takes about a day or so. It takes many months, or even years, of hard work to build one up.

The teams had finished labeling the steps on the process and were ready for some clarification.

"George, what is the percentage of value-added activities?"

"Let's see. There are thirty total stickies and four of them are value-added - so about thirteen percent."

"Excellent! So 87% of your process map is waste and has the potential to be eliminated.

"Next step: look at your household process and make a list of the wastes. Don't try to solve them at this point. Just make a note of them."

While the team was thinking about their wastes, I began thinking about the circle exercise that the sensei had me perform. During the Friday before my kaizen, he escorted me to the shop floor area that was the scope of my kaizen. There was a rough circle taped to the concrete floor and, through the translator, he directed me to stand in it. He gave me a sheet of paper and told me to keep writing down wastes until he returned. I remember being there for about an hour and again through the translator he said, "Good, now always stand in the circle where ever you go." I remember thinking it was silly at the time, but now having accountability for an entire site I realized he had given me some perspective.

The first team had the following list:

Washing & Drying Laundry Wastes

	Waste	Type
1	Walking to get laundry soap	Motion
2	Walking to get dryer sheets	Motion
3	Moving laundry from hamper to machine	Transportation
4	Washing towels when socks are needed	Overproduction
5	Moving laundry from washer to dryer	Transportation
6	Moving soap and dryer sheets back to cabinet	Transportation
7	Accidently placing a red sock in the white laundry	Defect

Johnny looked a bit confused and said, "Most of this stuff is related to the setup; is that right?"

"Yes," I said. "Setups are ripe with opportunity. In many cases, It is all about setup. Does anyone here play golf?"

Enrique, the QC technician, said, "Yes, I play about four times a week."

"Ok, great. How long does it take you to play a game if you walk the course?"

"Depending on the course, probably three or four hours."

"During that four hour game of golf, the head of the club is in contact with the ball for less than two seconds! Everything else is just set up for that minute activity."

I moved on to my next slide.

Week-long Kaizen Event
❑ Take a picture of the process to spot the waste ❑ Try-storm countermeasures to remove the waste

"What was the main waste associated with the material handling process from production's respect?"

Frankie said, "It was waiting waste, right? According to Johnny, there was a significant amount of waiting waste."

"Very good! Does anyone know what the waste of the process is from the logistics perspective?"

Johnny spoke up, but didn't seem too sure of himself when he said, "Is it defect waste? Occasionally we have been brought incorrect material."

Steve looked quite a bit irritated; his passion for excellence was becoming more apparent every single day.

Steve quipped, "That isn't necessarily the waste that affects you only. It is affecting both of our departments. I have to have my team make the pick again and then I spend hours sorting through the inventory discrepancy or other cause of the problem. You get increased waiting waste as the main problem."

"Interesting dialogue regarding the wastes of the process, but that is not the main one. The waste is transportation."

George chimed in, curious. "I'm extremely confused. How are moving the raw materials from the warehouse to the reaction area waste? We absolutely have to do it to make product."

"You have to have raw materials, but does Steve's team have to bring them to you?"

George responded, "Yes. Well… maybe I could have Johnny's team go get them, but the new system is working. I'm confused."

A light bulb simultaneously went off in Johnny and Steve's head.

They both started talking over each other, but Johnny won and said, "Could the supplier bring the material directly to the line?"

Steve smirked and said, "Could we set up an andon down the highway at the catalyst company?"

"We absolutely could ask. We have to understand that we are a customer as well and our vendors should at least be open to ideas such as this. We must rethink our business and understand that nothing is off of the table. More on this process of supplier management will be discussed later, but the concept is that we are customers and our countermeasures must be significant and they are not necessarily straight forward."

Sara raised her hand slowly. "So what is try-storming?" she asked.

"I was waiting for someone to ask that question. When the team suggests an idea that you all agree is appropriate, what is the process for implementing it? Let us assume it is a physical change to the process and not a policy or procedural change."

"Oh wow. First we have a design review to talk about the idea for an hour. Second we have all of the team members sign off on the change. We enter a maintenance work order to start the process. We may have to get corporate safety to sign off on the process, depending on whether or not it meets the requirements specified on checklist 4.5.1b." Sara rattled off the details, very familiar with the winding route any change was subject to.

"That type of process is very typical in American companies. A significant amount time is spent developing an idea that may or may not work. Lots of brainstorming is involved. Try-storming is what the Japanese sensei taught me. He literally went onto the floor with some duct-tape and cardboard to make a mockup of a system before starting the process of implementation. The mentality is that they would rather be on the floor testing than in the design room sketching."

Sara looked frustrated. "But we have to have these meetings to keep people safe. Our company requires them. We cannot simply 'try-storm' here," she complained.

"The first thing that you told me when I arrived was that you were having a lot of injuries already. I contend to you that having a practice run or a mock up would be significantly safer than not having one. Certainly you would want to have a safety briefing with management on the floor and discuss possible issues or safety concerns; maybe you would even draft a simple procedure for the team. I wouldn't squander more than an hour. In general you know about 50% of the issues that will occur while designing a new process. The other 50% of design problems won't be realized until we get out on the floor."

"Remember what happened with our last capital project?" George interjected. "It was a catastrophe. They ended up firing the project engineer and selling the equipment as scrap. He never left the office."

Johnny, impatient to find the answer, asked, "Ok, so we have to try-storm, but what are some examples of specific countermeasures, other than an andon system?"

"We will discuss the other tools in time. A great deal of companies trying to become lean simply focus on the tool. The tools are not the key; the key is to create a culture that is on a quest to eliminate waste from their processes in the spirit of 100% customer satisfaction."

"I guess I will accept that for now…I'm just used to having specific actions to take in situations like this," Johnny replied.

Time for the next slide.

Week-long Kaizen Event

- ❑ Take a picture of the process to spot the waste
- ❑ Try-storm countermeasures to remove the waste
- ❑ Put systems in place to sustain the countermeasures

"After you have identified the waste, we must put countermeasures in place to prevent the waste from returning. Wastes have a way of creeping back in to the operations process over time. The systems that we utilize must be resistant to complacency and degradation. Does anyone know if the material handling system will be resistant to degradation?"

Johnny responded, "Yes it will. We have a simple process that is easy to teach. Plus, it is beneficial to the customer and supplier."

"Those are true statements, but they won't necessarily keep the process pure. In actuality, within six months we could lose what we have gained because of one reason only: standard work. Standard work is the glue that holds the process together."

Steve added, "We talked about this in the training I went to. We need visual work instructions and/or standard operating procedures that ensure that everyone is doing the job the exact same way."

"Very good! If we don't put these items in place we will begin to backslide."

"I don't understand. I trained everyone with Steve's help. We are good to go," Johnny retorted.

"What is the common denominator to all organizations?"

"The people in them invariably change," George intoned.

I went to my next slide

Standard Work Implementation Process

- ❑ Define the standard
- ❑ Train to the standard
- ❑ Assess to the standard
- ❑ Kaizen the standard

"Johnny, you have done an excellent job of defining the standard verbally. The process is working! We need to define the standard in a documented manner. Here are some ways to document standardization:

Ways to Define/Document Standard Work

- ❑ Checklists
- ❑ Visual work instructions
  - – Lots of pictures
  - – As few words as possible
- ❑ Photos
- ❑ Videos of associates performing tasks
- ❑ Flow charts
- ❑ Worksheets
- ❑ Forms

"There is no right method to document standard work. That said, there are certainly better ways for different types of work. I wouldn't use a form or video for the material handling process."

"I still don't quite understand why this is better than on-the-job training." Johnny was still not quite on board with the concept.

"It is not that it is better. Standard work complements OJT. Think of it as OJT 2.0. A great example of standard work is Ray Kroc and the McDonalds system. Ray Kroc knew that employee turnover was high in the fast-food hamburger business. He wanted a way to bring new associates up to speed quickly. There is a defined progression that associates are trained in at McDonalds and many tasks at McDonalds have visual work instructions. There are also visual quality controls. At every McDonalds, above the fryer, there is a picture of underdone, overdone, and perfect French fries. I don't know if McDonalds uses lean and kaizen, but the French fries on the West Coast taste *exactly* the same as the French fries on the East Coast. That's the epitome of standardization."

Johnny, who still seemed a bit frustrated, said, "But our employees are a higher caliber than fast-food employees; this is a chemical factory."

George had his own answer. "That doesn't mean we shouldn't make their jobs simpler. Think of how much money we have spent on hazardous waste disposal because an associate did steps out of sequence. If we had visual work instructions, maybe we would have not failed all of those batches!"

"Excellent. You are getting it! Remember standard work is OJT 2.0! Once the standard is in place, we must ensure that the standard is being followed. This could be a formal audit program or as simple as a manager working side by side with a line associate. One word of caution: if we decide to use a formal audit program we will always use a front-line associate as an 'auditing partner.' I have found that having an army of managers with clipboards and audit sheets leads to animosity among the line associates and could become a labor relations issue if sustained."

"I like the idea of every associate doing every task the exact same way," Sara interposed. "It will make managing the safety performance much simpler. Everyone will have on the same personal protective equipment and do the steps in same order."

"Our last step is to kaizen the standard. We must get our team in a frame of mind that the standard can always be changed. In fact, we should encourage it. The standardization cycle will become like thawing and refreezing an ice cube. Does anyone have any questions?"

"Yes," said Johnny. "When do we have our first kaizen?"

"We have a bit more training to do first; we are almost ready."

13. POPPING A CURIOUS QUESTION

I had gotten in the habit of running weekly plant meetings with the entire site. This simple exercise can help the culture significantly. I often refer to it as ubiquitous communication. In general, people get nervous or afraid when things are changing and there is no communication regarding the changes. Years later, I had a supervisor ask me if we should have a weekly meeting when there was no new information to put out. He was missing the point of the meeting. The flow of information is secondary to spending quality time with your team. Make sure to err on the side of over communication during a rapid change cycle or after a kaizen event.

During one of my plant meetings I received a curious comment that I had not thought of before. This concept was so totally foreign to me, and everything I stood for, that the question genuinely caught me off guard.

Tucker was a seasoned employee with well over twenty five years of service. He had literally moved with the plant three times until finally settling in its current location.

He raised his hand toward the end of the meeting. "We keep talkin' 'bout all of these improvements. I'm scared that I am going to be improved right out of a job. We have less than half of the people here that we did ten years ago."

Again, I was taken aback by the remark. I paused for a few seconds to gather my thoughts. In the meantime, Tucker looked a little bit smug.

"I can't speak for what has been done in the past; what I can do is discuss our strategy going forward. My goal for our site is to make us the highest performing and best service level chemical plant. First we want to be the best in the American region. Next, we want to be the best in our company. After that, we want to propagate our system out to other sites in our company."

Tucker interrupted me and started to get heated. "What does that have to do with my job?"

I motioned to Johnny to go get me an easel from the conference room and some markers.

"I'm getting to that; I promise. Let me ask a question first while I am waiting for the board. Has anyone ever bought anything that they were unsatisfied with?"

The room let out a laugh and I chuckled myself because obviously it was a ridiculous question.

"Let me first propose you a question about customer satisfaction. What is more likely to cause you to stop shopping from a vendor: habitual late delivery or low quality?"

There was a murmur in the room as they thought it over. The team arrived at about a 70/30 consensus, with late delivery ahead.

"That's a fair guess. A customer is actually five times more likely to leave because of a bad process, like a late delivery, than a bad product. Think about going to your local grocery store. If you got a bad gallon of milk one time, you will probably return the milk and get a new one; this may happen more than once. If you show up to a grocery store and there is no milk twice in a row, the chances of you returning to the store when you are just looking to pick up milk is slim to none."

I drew a sketch up on the easel:

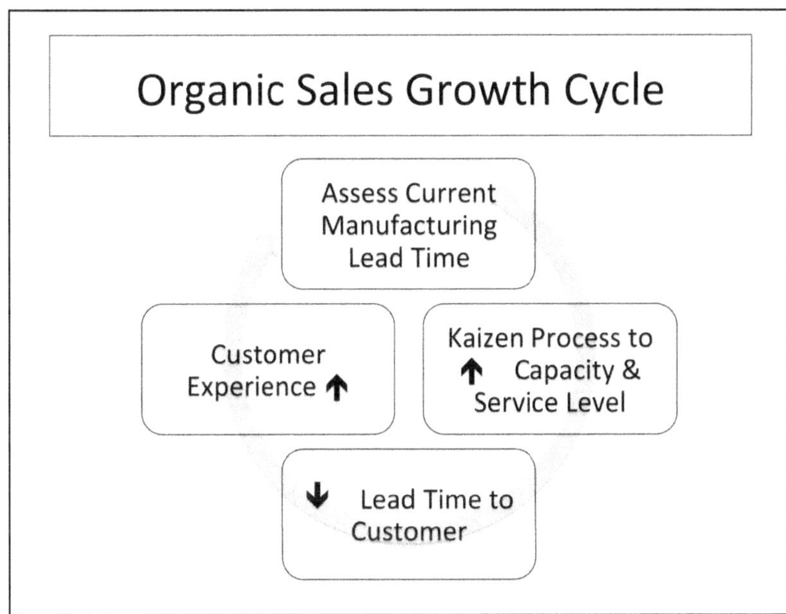

"What we must achieve is a cycle of organic sales growth by increasing our service level to the customers. We can absolutely drive the sales increases by simply improving our customer satisfaction. As we increase customer satisfaction, our customers will buy more of our product; this is especially true in our industry because we are a second source to some downstream manufacturers that use our product as raw material."

Tucker started to speak up but I cut him off; I don't generally do that, but I needed some more time to make my points.

"The volume of production out of this plant has been flat or decreased for the last seven years. The only way the company can make more money is to cut expenses. What we need to do is increase the sales so we can keep everyone employed and maybe even hire more people. We want to help the social aspect of the economy, not take away from it."

Everyone seemed to be set at ease after that answer. I genuinely believed what I was telling the team, but I knew Devon would not be on board. Decreasing the headcount at the plants was his top priority. We were literally going to have to accomplish improvements by the next budget cycle and grow the business in less than twelve months.

Selecting the Target Process

The next morning I pulled the leadership team into the conference room for a discussion regarding the kaizen event.

"Team, the reason I have pulled you guys together again is so we can select the process we're going to improve."

I flashed up the following slide onto the projector:

"So all of you have been to kaizen leader training. I am still a 'stranger' to the plant. The only thing I am going to do is pick our kaizen leader. The rest of the leadership team and front-line associates are going to drive the improvements. During the event, I will be tech support only. The first kaizen leader is going to be Johnny."

George smirked and exclaimed, "Speech! Speech! He wishes he had time for preparing an acceptance speech."

Johnny had a big smile, but decided not to say anything. It was obvious that he was very pleased with himself.

"I selected Johnny because he has a thirst for lean thinking and tools. He has a respect for his team and he has managed every production process in the building over his five years of service."

Next slide:

First Kaizen Selection Guidelines
❑ It is best to have the first kaizen leader "pre-selected" and that leader should be intimately familiar with that process ❑ Selected process should have a large financial impact to the business

"Why would we want the process to have a large financial impact to the company?"

"Because we are in the business of making money?" Steve tentatively replied.

"Yes, that is true; however, currently, I am not in the business of making money. Right now I am in the business of improving our processes."

Johnny interjected, "Yes, but isn't kaizen and process improvement going to help us make money?"

"Yes, that's true, but right now we have to prove to the corporate organization that our methodology of process improvements is going to help create a sustainable business. When kaizen leaders set goals for improvement during an event, they are always stretch goals. When we run the first kaizen, I am going to expect you to *double or half all target metrics.*"

George literally dropped his jaw after hearing the stretch goal criteria.

Johnny immediately said, "You expect me to half my cycle time or double my throughput." His anxiety level seemed to skyrocket at the thought.

"After I spent the day working with Dave on the main reactor, I genuinely believe you could triple the throughput with no capital investment; however, I think doubling would be a good goal."

"I'm not an engineer; I'm just not smart enough to do that magnitude of improvement." Johnny started to list all the reasons he felt he would fail.

Johnny had been a victim of bad programming his entire life. He had a low self-esteem, but covered it very well. I would later find out that his dad abandoned his family when he was about ten.Johnny never went to college in order to take the burden off of his mother; he enabled his little brother to go instead. I respected him a great deal for his sacrifice and dedication to his family.

"Johnny, you don't have to be an engineer. You have to engage your associates and attack the waste. With proper team selection, you will hit a home run. I promise!"

He smiled, but still didn't seem sure of himself. I went ahead and explained my reasoning for criteria one. "We want to select a high financial gain target so that the upper management will see the value of kaizen. If we improve a process 30% that generated $200,000 in revenue we only get a small gain. If we improve the process 30% that has $20,000,000 in revenue the management will literally come down to see what we are doing."

I flashed up my last slide.

First Kaizen Selection Guidelines

- ❑ It is best to have the first kaizen leader "pre-selected" and that leader should be intimately familiar with that process
- ❑ Selected process should have a large financial impact to the business
- ❑ Try to select a labor intensive process that requires substantial amount of "touches"

"Third criteria: we want to select a process with a good potential for improvement. The best processes have manual characteristics such as loading or setup time. We probably do not want to select highly automated processes because, in general, their waste is harder to affect on a short timetable. This is only for the first kaizen. The first kaizen is sacred; we want to ensure that the team is successful so that we can have a positive cultural impact. We will tackle automated process, but not for the first kaizen.

"Does anyone have any suggestions? Remember I'm the new guy; I don't necessarily know what needs to be fixed. You have all the experience."

The normally quiet Frankie spoke out. "The packaging lines give us so many problems. It's very automated but no thought was put into obtaining a good design."

George got a bit heated. "Yes, but our packaging line isn't slowing us down. Even with the problems we have on the packaging lines, we could run it on about two and a quarter shifts and cover our volume. Our main reactor is the constraint."

George went to the white board and drew the following sketch:

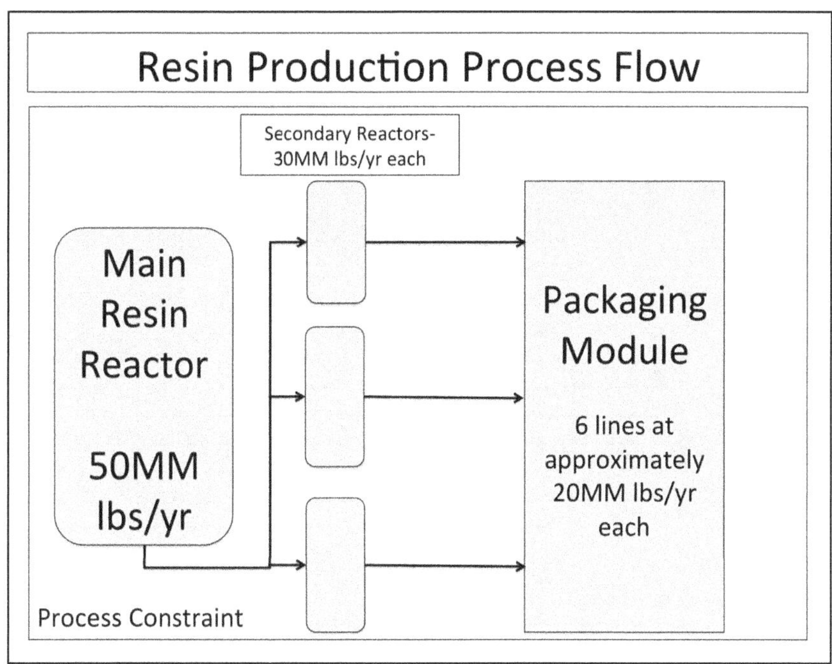

George continued, "If we could get the main reactor up to even 90 million pounds per year, we could seriously push the bottleneck to the packaging module and increase throughput. *Then* we can work on the packaging lines that are giving us the most problems."

"Excellent! Does anyone have any issues with tackling the main reactor as our first kaizen event?"

Everyone looked excited, anxious, and worried all at the same time. We were reaching out into an unknown territory. I have seen this done before, but it was the fake lean system. We were either going to fail big or win bigger. There would be no lukewarm answer to this question.

"Ok Johnny. We need a few things before the event:

1. Put a sign-up list for team members in the break room.
2. We need 2-4 target metrics for the event.
3. We need a snap shot of the current state for those metrics."

I passed out the following handout:

Kaizen Event Target Sheet

Event Description (work center)	Event Dates
Main Reactor Product A- 60% of volume	2/12-2/16

	Current	Target	Day 1	Day 2	Day 3	Day 4	Final	% Δ
Cycle time								
Volume per day								
Space (sq. ft.)								
Inventory								
Walking distance								
Transport distance								
Changeover time								
Quality improvements								
Visual controls								
Safety improvements								

CULTURALKAIZEN Kaizen Event Target Sheet

"We are going to meet a week from today to select the team and go over the target metrics."

As the meeting broke, Johnny hung back for a few minutes so we could have a chat.

Johnny asked, "Do you really think we can get this done?"

"Absolutely. We will get a big win out of this. Picking the team and the proper pre-work will be crucial for us."

"I guess I will have to wait and see," Johnny answered.

"Just take this one on faith. Running a kaizen will be the toughest thing you have ever done. You are going to be under pressure more than you ever have before. You will be triumphant and successful. The entire experience will grow you!"

"Alright, I will get the target sheet together and see you next week."

14. THREE WEEKS BEFORE 1ST KAIZEN EVENT

I had decided to come in to work a bit early one day to spend some time with the night shift before our first pre-kaizen meeting. Something interesting had happened as I passed through the gate. Marcos flagged me to stop.

"How are you doing today sir? I have a quick question for you. What is a kay-zen? All of the guys keep talking about this kay-zen thing that they are signing up for."

I chuckled. "We are just trying to make it a better place to work."

"Fair enough, sir. Whatever you are doing, the team seems happy about it. Maybe we will get bonuses next year after all!"

"I hope that we do!"

I didn't even realize that the team hadn't received their holiday bonuses. Devon had struck again! I was none-the-wiser and no one wanted to bring it up to me. We still had a ways to go with the culture.

Later that morning I sat down with Johnny, George, and Kellen. Kellen wasn't specifically asked for in the scope of the pre-work meeting, but he wanted to be a part of the lean transformation. My perception was that he hadn't made much traction as a process engineer and was hoping he could turn the corner.

"Johnny, the first thing we have to do is pick out our kaizen team. This is one of the most important steps in running the kaizen. There are ten major kaizen pitfalls that have to be avoided; four of them have to do with team selection. We have to get this ironed out."

Johnny wrote the sign-up list on the white board as follows:

Kaizen Event Sign-up List

1. Dave- 1st shift Main Reactor Operator
2. Stacy- 2nd shift Main Reactor Operator
3. Nick- PVC Lead Operator
4. Enrique- Lab Tech
5. Clarence- Operator- worked all units
6. Trevor-1st Shift Warehouse Operator
7. Glenn- 2nd Shift Warehouse Operator
8. Carl- 1st Shift Solvent Operator
9. Daniel O- 2nd Shift Solvent Operator
10. Sammy- 2nd Shift Solvent Operator
11. Scott M- 2nd Shift Maintenance Tech
12. Doug- 1st shift Resin Packaging Operator
13. Aaron-3rd shift Resin Packaging Operator

Johnny asked the first question. "What is a good number of people to have on the team?"

George chimed in, "I would think no more than eight people."

"Definitely no more than that. Additionally, I think we should go with Johnny, plus five others for the first event. It is a bigger risk improperly managing eight people than not having enough team members to get the job done. I doubt that, in this economy, they will mind working overtime if we need them to."

George responded, "It still amazes me that you aren't concerned about managing the cost like everyone else is. Overtime is like a cardinal sin in the eyes of upper management."

"I'm good with six. I am concerned, though: only three people signed up that have significant experience running the main reactor," Johnny said.

"Why is that a problem?"

"The main reactor takes months to learn how to run properly. I just hope we have enough brain power on the team to compensate."

George said, "Johnny, I don't think that is necessarily a bad thing. We want people who haven't accepted status quo to help you improve the process."

"That's an excellent point, George. Johnny, as one of our team selection constraints, you may only have one of the main reactor operators on your team. The level of improvements that the kaizen process generates is going to take a new brand of thinking."

Johnny said, "Alright, then I take Dave as the reactor operator for the team. You seem to have built a rapport with him and he is one of my guys that is looked up to the most. He should be able to help us get the changes in place."

"You have the option of taking a co-lead for the event. It isn't required, but it will serve two purposes. First, if you need to break into sub-teams, you will have a go-to person. Second, we will be training the co-lead to be the next kaizen leader."

Johnny said, "I pick Enrique from the lab."

Kellen said, "That's an interesting choice. Why did you pick him?"

"He is a natural leader and he is always helping out. He can do anything from report production to run the unit. Plus he has a positive attitude coupled with a competitive spirit!" Johnny said.

I appreciated the thought process behind Johnny's decision. "Well, you have me sold! He will be our co-lead. I would recommend taking a maintenance technician. I am betting you will have some physical changes involved with your event. Taking a maintenance tech will help get buy-in from the maintenance team, give you constant technical support during the event, and will help break down the typical maintenance versus production rivalry."

Specific Cultural Nuances

In any operations environment there will be challenges unique to that particular industry. However, there are some challenges that remain constant regardless of organization type.

Two of these cultural challenges are *functional friction* and *inter-shift rivalry*. Functional friction exists between departments to some degree at most major organizations. An example of this in a manufacturing or operations organization is a conflict between production (operations) and maintenance functions. Anyone who has spent any amount of time working in either environment has heard process operators complaining about equipment that doesn't run correctly and, conversely, maintenance technicians present the argument that production continues to break it. The problem exists due to a lack of ownership. Production is traditionally held accountable for getting product "out the back door;" maintenance is held accountable for "keeping the equipment in good working order." (This relationship exists between other support functions and operations as well, e.g. human resources, sales, safety, finance, etc.)

Strategies For Minimizing Functional Friction

- Cross-functional Training: Incorporate cross-functional training into the onboarding process. Having support staff spend a few weeks in each operational area is time and money well spent. The same goes for operations staff as well.

- Cross-functional Goals: All functions should be held accountable for revenue creation in some shape or form. Referring back to the maintenance technician example, maintenance managers can be held accountable for production targets. If managed properly, this will have a collaborative effect between production and maintenance.

The other area that ubiquitously exists in production (operations) environments is *inter-shift rivalry*. Multi-shift operation is occurring more and more frequently in today's changing economy. Multi-shift operations provide for better asset utilization when large capital expenditures are not viable options for many companies. Front-line managers are your best defense and detection that inter-shift rivalry is building.

Signs Of Inter-shift Rivalry

- ❖ Complaints by team members that a specific shift isn't "pulling their weight."

  Note: Complaints are traditionally heard during managers' normal working hours. Beware, a potential bias can be created by first (day) shift regarding the other shifts' behaviors.

- ❖ Exclusion of off-shift team members during company activities/ team meetings.

- ❖ Setting the next shift up for failure (purposely or through neglect).

Strategies For Mitigating Inter-Shift Rivalry

- ❖ Inter-shift Communication: Communication between shifts is paramount. If twenty four hour coverage is utilized, it is well worth the time required by having a shift to shift transition. During the changeover meeting the biggest thing that needs to be covered is exception reporting. There is an agreed upon standard (formal or informal) that each shift is responsible for; if the standard is not met due to operational considerations, the reason needs to be discussed during changeover.

  I have literally seen two opposite shift team members almost come to blows over the trash not being taken out. A little communication goes a long way!

- Team Based Performance Targets: Eliminate individual shift performance targets if possible. Having a production target of 1,000 widgets for each shift has the side effect of minimizing teamwork across shifts. A much better method is using daily targets such as 3,000 widgets per day. Then, the importance of setting the next team up for success can be emphasized much easier.

- Cross-shift teams: Give different team members the opportunity to work with people that they don't normally have access to. A kaizen event is a perfect time to get this done.

- Shift Rotation: Although this one can be taxing on management, it can be beneficial to have shift team members work different shifts over the course of their employment. Some companies rearrange shifts and departments every year effectively. Standard work and proper cross-training are doubly important if this strategy is utilized.

We went back and forth for about twenty more minutes until we had a good sample of the different functions in the building. We finally arrived with the following team:

First Kaizen Event Team
Focus: Main Reactor

1. Johnny- **Team Lead**
2. Enrique- Lab Tech **Co-Lead**
3. Dave- 1st shift Main Reactor Operator
4. Daniel O- 2nd Shift Solvent Operator
5. Trevor-1st Shift Warehouse Operator
6. Scott M- 2nd Shift Maintenance Tech

February 12-16 6am - 4pm
Food will be provided

"Great, make sure you post this after our meeting. The next thing we need to talk about is your target metrics for the event."

Johnny handed us slides for our event.

Johnny's Kaizen Event Target Sheet

Event Description (work center) Main Reactor Product A- 60% of volume	Event Dates 2/12-2/16

	Current	Target	Day 1	Day 2	Day 3	Day 4	Final	% Δ
Cycle time	12 hrs	9 hrs						
Volume per day								
Space (sq. ft.)								
Inventory								
Walking distance								
Transport distance								
Changeover time	2	1.5						
Quality improvements								
Visual controls	0	2						
Safety improvements								

Kaizen Event Target Sheet

"First, let's go over why you selected each of your target metrics. Walk me through your thought process."

Johnny said, "Ok. Here goes. I picked cycle time because cycle time directly relates to how fast we can get product out of the door. If we decrease the cycle time than we can make more batches of product."

"That's a true statement. Remember, if we don't take that reduced cycle time and translate it into more direct batches, then we have done nothing. I have seen instances of reduced cycle time not resulting in more products out the door or improved service level. It shouldn't be an issue; we just need to be conscious of it. Alright, what's next?"

"The second metric I selected was changeover time. Cleaning, purging, and loading the reactor take a great deal of time. It could be up to six hours, but the average is about two. We used to combat this by trying to changeover less. I have been reading some of the books you suggested and I finally get what Steve has been trying to tell me all these years."

"What was he trying to tell you?"

"The way I was running the schedule was delaying our customer shipments. We want to figure out how to reduce the changeover time so we can service the customers better."

"Excellent! Please continue."

Johnny seemed pleased with the conversation so far. "The last two metrics are visual controls and safety. We don't have any visual controls and I like the way the material handling system is working. I think we need more controls to make the process flow better. The safety goal is associated with an injury we had. One of the operators had an injury falling down the ladder a few years ago. They have to go up and down the ladder between ten and twenty times to prepare one batch or change over the reactor."

"Those are good observations. Remember though, we don't want to create waste from visual controls. Only use them if they help the process. Alright, let's talk numbers now!"

After I looked the sheet over and observed that the cycle time goal was not what I expected, I asked a simple question. "What are you afraid of?"

Johnny looked puzzled and said, "What do you mean?"

"I know you remember me telling you that we needed to double or half everything as a target metric. What's the problem? What do I need to do?"

George stepped in. "I just don't think either of us see how we can cut a twelve hour cycle time down to six hours. Both of us thought nine would be great."

"I agree nine would be great. If you guys use nine as a goal, the team will think little tiny ideas and we might get a one-hour reduction. If you set a cycle time goal of six hours, then the team will come up with new and radical ideas."

The target sheet should look like this:

Revised Kaizen Event Target Sheet

Event Description (work center)	Event Dates
Main Reactor Product A- 60% of volume	2/12-2/16

	Current	Target	Day 1	Day 2	Day 3	Day 4	Final	% Δ
Cycle time	12	6						
Volume per day								
Space (sq. ft.)								
Inventory								
Walking distance								
Transport distance								
Changeover time (hours)	2	1						
Quality improvements								
Visual controls	0	2						
Safety improvements								

CULTURALKAIZEN Kaizen Event Target Sheet

Johnny and George still looked concerned, but it was something they were going to have to learn to accept. Obviously I would be pleased if we were able to obtain a 25% cycle time reduction and corresponding throughput increase, but we could not start off planning to fail.

Lean Learnings: If your team sets little goals, they will produce little ideas. If your team selects big goals, they will produce big ideas!

"Alright, does anyone else have any questions before we break?"

Johnny still wasn't convinced on the cycle time reduction goal. "What makes you so sure that we will be successful?"

"All manufacturing facilities are the same. They bring stuff in the front door, change it, and ship it out of the back door. This facility, like many others, has never had the front-line team map out the process to identify the waste. Once we teach them to do that, we will be unstoppable. We are no longer in the chemicals business; we are in the business of improving our processes!"

Ten Kaizen Pitfalls

Concept: The framework of kaizen events is relatively fluid depending on the operations, strategy, culture, and leadership of an organization. The pitfalls are an absolute constant!

Pitfall 10: Improper Team Selection A: Management Bias. Everyone remembers picking teams for sports in school. The athletic children were always snagged first; the nerds were always picked last (big surprise). The tendency of a team leader to select the best candidates is a natural but dangerous one; obviously, we want to succeed. Anyone who has fallen victim to this pitfall will not feel its effects until *after* the kaizen. Under most circumstances, the kaizen event will be an earth-shattering success. The final report out will show kaizen stretch goals as blips in the teams rear-view mirror. This pitfall is a cultural time-bomb!

The bomb was set if the team list was posted as follows:

Area A supervisor
Area B supervisor
Area C supervisor
Maintenance manager
In-bound operations manager
Process engineer
Token front-line associate

The front-line team now views kaizen as a management scheme to force new changes into the organization. If this is the site's first kaizen, it is unlikely it will recover. There will simply be no buy-in.

Pitfall 9: Improper Team Selection B: Improper Functional Cross-section. A natural tendency of the team leader and project chair is to stack the deck with the most functional knowledge possible.

The team list was posted as follows:

Project Scope: Turbine Generator and Auxiliary Systems:

A-Shift Turbine Operator
C-Shift Turbine Operator
A-Shift Auxiliary Operator
Reactor -Turbine Maintenance Manager
Turbine Area Day front-line manager

The problem with this team is a subtle one. The likelihood of getting a marginal (5-10%) improvement is very high, but the rapid step-change improvement is not going to come to fruition. The aforementioned team knows the process better than any other people on site. So what is wrong with that? The chance that they are going to question the status quo is slim. They will generate ideas that are small tweaks or automation of existing process. The changes will work, but are unlikely to have a larger ROI.

Pitfall 8: Improper Team Selection C: Various.

These are small errors in team composition that are hindrances to culture or buy-in of the changes.

- Representation by only one shift/portion of the site.
- All passive team members. It is not a requirement to have all influencers or all drivers on the team. In fact, it is a good development opportunity for less vocal team members to gain some assertiveness! That being said, a team leader's worst nightmare is having a team of six where no one is talking.
- Perceived favoritism or discrimination.

Pitfall 7: Improper Team Leader Selection. Selecting a team leader (and co-lead if necessary) can be the event's greatest asset or biggest challenge. There are several things to consider when picking a team lead:

- Relationship to the project scope
- People Skills
    - Motivator
    - Communicator
    - Trainer
- Technical Skills
- Organizational Skills
- Open-minded

There are no hard and fast rules or specific personality types. Use your best judgment to avoid this one.

Pitfall 6: Inadequate Event Pre-work. There is specific set of pre-work items that need to be completed before the event takes place. Most sites have checklists or databases that exist to "ensure" the pre-work gets finished properly. I can't exactly explain what good pre-work and bad pre-work is; however, inadequate pre-work is just going through the motions. The solution to this pitfall is to have a seasoned project chair guiding the leader and meeting once a week prior to the event for

3-4 weeks.

Pitfall 5: Pre-solving the Kaizen. The other side of the pre-work pitfall is the motivated team leader that already has the solution made up in their mind before the event even starts. If the leader's idea works, then there is no harm in this pitfall. However, the more likely situation is that the singular idea will not work and the kaizen wasted hundreds of man-hours. This is a tricky one to avoid because your brain naturally wants to fill in the blanks of a problem. The best thing the team leader can do is not map out the process until the event starts. The value stream map generates most of the ideas for the solution, so resist the urge to start the map before the event.

Pitfall 4: Kaizen Hedgehog Solution. This pitfall occurs when the team has properly mapped out the process, but hangs their hat on one key change. This is simply a statistical problem. I would much rather have ten 3% changes than one 30% change. If only seven of the former group pan-out, you still have a 21% gain. I absolutely agree with Jim Collins, author of *Good to Great*, regarding having a hedgehog concept for the strategic vision of a company; however, during a kaizen, be the fox!

Pitfall 3: Inappropriate Scope. Having too big of a project or too small of a project will also prevent success. Most people know the basic functions of a distribution center.

Scoped too large: Outbound logistics
Scoped too small: Single carrier truck loading
Scoped right: Outbound dock and material handling

If you are confused about which side of the line to err, go with slightly too large.

Pitfall 2: Inadequate Team Training. The kaizen team needs to be properly prepared. Everyone on site should have basic "awareness" training of the kaizen process. The team leaders should receive 10-20 hours of focused training including a simulated Kaizen. The whole team should have an additional 3-6 hours of training before the event. I recommend doing team training on the Friday before an event. The team training should consist, at a minimum, of value stream mapping and basic lean tools.

And the number 1 kaizen pitfall is:

Pitfall 1: Inadequate Process Mapping. This one is going to be short, but it is absolutely the most important.

An inadequate process map has the following characteristics:

- Macro level process steps
- Small percentage of non-value added steps
- Doesn't consider all:
    - Activities
    - Connections
    - Flows
    - Materials
    - Information
- Takes less than 10 man-hours to complete
- The above process map took over 100 man-hours to construct
- Doesn't include individual action step cycle times- BoxTime™

Although, there are many kaizen event pitfalls, they can be easily dodged by the proper identification and controls. Unfortunately, I learned several of these pitfalls through experience. Some simple abatement questions you can ask are:

- How will this decision affect the culture of the plant?
- Have we consulted the front-line team about their opinion of the process changes? The process path

leaders?

- ❖ Is this methodology going to land me up in one of the kaizen pitfalls?

15. MOLE IN THE RANKS

It was about 7:30 pm and I had just put my son to sleep. I sat down to have my first bite of a lukewarm dinner when I saw my phone start to vibrate. I looked at the screen and I saw the following:

> **Devon Carpenter**
>
> **952-555-1212**

My wife, who was getting increasingly tired of being interrupted during dinner, scoffed and walked away.

I picked up the phone. "Hello."

"Good evening. Sorry to call so late. I have a few questions for you that can't wait until tomorrow."

"No problem. Go ahead." Actually, it was a bit of a problem, but I had decided to take the call and now had to live with the consequences.

"How have you been tracking against your key performance indicators that we talked about?"

In all honesty, I hadn't even been looking at them. We had a plan and we were executing to the plan. The KPIs are secondary. My mentors had always taught me that there are only two real metrics: injuries and profit dollars.

Everything else is superfluous. I have never been able to exchange hard earned productivity percentage points or inventory turns at the grocery store and bring home food. Many managers get into a metric/numbers driven trap and their subordinates start to "game" the numbers.

"We are on track." *Well, I thought we were.* Our morale had significantly improved and, although I could not quantify it, I had learned from experience that a step-change morale improvement would drive productivity up no less than ten percent.

"Please send me an updated tracking sheet showing your progress to the goals by next Friday."

"Very well." I would end up doing this myself because I did not want to bog any of my team down with anything other than the upcoming kaizen. Exposing them to the mass production mindset would be detrimental to the lean culture that was being developed.

"Also, can you tell me why you are shutting down the plant for a week to run an improvement event?"

WOW! I had a mole in the ranks. Devon had either called one of my team or they had reached out to him. I was hoping I wouldn't go through this kind of ordeal, but it seemed to be unavoidable at this point.

"Well, we aren't shutting down the unit exactly. We can't run a kaizen without having the unit running. We are springing a few operators from a shift and a supervisor to work on our constrained asset."

"This sounds like something your process engineer should be working on, not your operators."

That was one of the worst possible things that he could say to me. I finally figured him out. He placed next to zero value on the front-line associate. This was the reason that he could close so many plants and still sleep well at night. He treated them as tools to be used up and cast aside. It was sad really.

"I want team members like Kellen to be a part of our lean journey, but the process engineers are support staff. The line supervisors will become the process path leaders and the process engineers are tech support for them. We want the floor taking ownership of the changes. Regardless, I still understand that I have to be totally accountable for our KPIs and requirements."

"So what do you plan on doing after this kaizen week? Where are you going from there?"

"Well, my goal would be to have an event every single month, or at least six per year. Additionally we need to implement 5S to improve the housekeeping. These improvements have to come from the floor to drive the culture in a positive direction. If I am the one pushing the changes, then we will fail in the long term."

The conversation droned on for another thirty minutes or so. We kept "discussing" different points, but by the end I think we both realized that we weren't going to change each other's opinion.

Devon finally ended with, "I will be down there in about a month. We will discuss this further then. Please don't forget to send me a tracking sheet describing performance to the established KPIs."

"Ok, no problem! I will take care of it for you."

I got off the phone feeling extremely frustrated that one of my team had broken the ranks of sorts. I could only assume that the team member had been threatened in some way, shape, or form. I sent out a meeting request to my team and typed up a few slides. I needed to quell this now - we weren't at the point where we could survive a rebellion.

Time for a Mole Hunt

The team started sitting down at the conference room table and there didn't seem to be anyone straggling in for a change. I wonder if word got about regarding Devon's information about the kaizen.

"Last night I received a call from Devon asking me about the kaizen event we are going to be running in a few weeks. Does anyone know anything about that? He caught me really off guard."

I saw no reason to pull punches. I was hoping that someone would have some backbone. Unfortunately, no one had any information to give me. I decided to use my plan B.

"George, how many different measurements did you have last year?"

George sighed. "I think about seven or eight different measures," he said.

"It was at least ten," Steve interjected. "I remember having a beer with you complaining about what kind of impossible task focusing on ten metrics would be."

"That is true. I remember saying the goals filled up two whole hands," George replied.

"So obviously both of you realize there are an incredible amount of differences in lean manufacturing versus traditional manufacturing?"

I got some head nods, but nothing definitive.

I flashed up my first slide.

Comparison of Two Mentalities

Traditional Manufacturing	Lean Manufacturing
1. You make profit through maximum utilization of your resources	1. You make profit by maximizing the flow to your customers

"Does anyone have any thoughts on this first point?"

George said, "Isn't it a waste to have machines idle? Shouldn't we maximize the uptime on them to make more money?"

"Let me propose a question; does it make sense to run your TV twenty four hours a day when you sleep eight?"

Everyone giggled, because it was an over simplification, but it absolutely made sense.

"George, our goal is to match capacity to demand. We should run only when we need to. The reason to improve the processes is so that we have to run less to meet demand. If you think about the entire supply chain, we want to push the constraint out into the marketplace."

Lean Learnings: Having excess capacity gives the sales & marketing team the ability to move more product. The capacity must come first; otherwise, you are setting your customers up for dissatisfaction.

I segued into my next slide.

Comparison of Two Mentalities

Traditional Manufacturing	Lean Manufacturing
1. You make profit through maximum utilization of your resources	1. You make profit by maximizing the flow to your customers
2. Direct labor is the main cost you focus on eliminating	2. Waste is what we focus on eliminating

"Can anyone tell me about the second statement on the left side of the screen?"

"Yes." George said, "We have a goal of reducing headcount every year. When I did the last budget cycle that was the main topic of discussion; we looked at full time equivalent in the first budget cycle and then what the FTE would look like after re-budgeting. The whole process was frustrating because if we didn't let those two people go, we would have been able to ship product more effectively. It only ended up 'saving' us around $125,000 per year, but probably cost us five times that in top-line business. We are basically in a one-step forward, one-step back machine."

George had pretty much covered all of the points I wanted to make, so I went on to the next slide.

Comparison of Two Mentalities

Traditional Manufacturing	Lean Manufacturing
1. You make profit through maximum utilization of your resources	1. You make profit by maximizing the flow to your customers
2. Direct labor is the main cost you focus on eliminating	2. Waste is what we focus on eliminating
3. The business system is controlled through metrics and extremely detailed tracking	3. The business is controlled thru continuous attention to flow & waste

"So who got tired of filling out reports over the last year or so?"

About half of the room raised their hands. I think the other half was either scared or lying.

"Based on my conversations with Devon, it's pretty obvious where the focus has been; this *must* change. The focus has to be in the gemba looking at the flows of the floor and identifying waste. As long as we keep eliminating waste, we will get better and better. The numbers will take care of themselves completely!"

Comparison of Two Mentalities

Traditional Manufacturing	Lean Manufacturing
1. You make profit through maximum utilization of your resources	1. You make profit by maximizing the flow to your customers
2. Direct labor is the main cost you focus on eliminating	2. Waste is what we focus on eliminating
3. The business system is controlled through metrics and extremely detailed tracking	3. The business is controlled thru continuous attention to flow & waste
4. Excess capacity is detrimental to business	4. Excess capacity provides flexibility to serve our customers more completely and variably

"To me, this one applies most to our business system. I have seen a chart that directly correlates FTE to capacity level. It seems counterintuitive, but we *want* people to be standing around. If they are not busy they can work on improving the process even further *and* the constraint has been shifted to the marketplace."

Sara begrudgingly raised her hand and said, "It was me. I called him. Please forgive me. I am so sorry."

"Don't worry. It will be ok. We just have to hit a homerun for sure now, because the kaizen must bear fruit or we will get shut down. Johnny is going to make us proud!"

"There is nothing like adding a little bit of gasoline to the fire. It will work! We will make it happen!" Johnny encouraged the team.

"I will talk to you tomorrow. Two weeks left until the first event!"

16. HORIZONTAL VS. VERTICAL

Sara poked her head inside my office early the next morning, almost in tears.

"Come on in. What can I do for you?"

Her lip began to quiver as she spoke. "I'm terribly sorry for what I did to you. I wish I could take it back now."

"You really didn't do anything to me personally, but it is going to be tough driving our changes horizontally across the other business units. Also, we will have less margin for error overall. We are basically going to have to hit a bull's-eye on the first try. I am curious, though; what made you call him?"

She pondered her reply for a few minutes. "I just feel like what you are selling us is magic beans. We have been working at this plant for years and years. Suddenly, you come on board and start telling us that everything we are doing is wrong and that having the operators participate is the key to our success. Most of them have only graduated high school and a few of them haven't even done that. How are they smarter than us?"

I intentionally waited for a bit before responding to Sara. I did not want her to think that I wasn't listening to her. Her objection, although not valid from a lean and kaizen viewpoint, is absolutely valid from a traditional, mass production one.

"The issue you are speaking of has little to do from an education standpoint. Regardless of our training, occupation, or function, we can all understand macro level concepts of our processes."

"For example?" she demanded quickly.

"You are a safety professional. You absolutely understand that operators must put on a full-face respirator when loading raw material that could release organic vapors. The operators know this as well. The difference is that you can tell me every minute OSHA requirement governing the proper care, storage, and maintenance of respirators. You also might be able to tell me *why* we chose a particular vapor cartridge. If you are really heavy into industrial hygiene, you may even be able to tell me how the cartridge chemically separates the toxic vapors from the rest of the air while still allowing enough fresh air to pass to allow the worker to breathe. This is true, correct?"

Steve had previously filled me in that she worked in industrial hygiene for the largest chemical company in the US but changed jobs when her husband relocated. This was a good time to use that golden nugget. Sara went into a diatribe about respirators and their function in many gasses that we used, and even some we did not. I had to reel her back in after about five minutes; I didn't see her slowing down anytime soon.

"Now, how many times per shift does each operator put a respirator on?"

She looked at me, puzzled. "I don't know that. I would have to ask them."

"Exactly! Our job is not to do the work for them. Our job is to support them in their work. The work that I am proposing that they engage in is going to change from simply producing chemicals to improving the chemical production process first and producing chemicals second. All I want us to do is empower them to make the process better. We will do this hand in hand; however, the improvement should generally come from the front-line first. We are always going to have large, strategic process changes and those will be top-down, but at least 80% of our improvement efforts should come directly from the front line. Let me show you a generic organization chart."

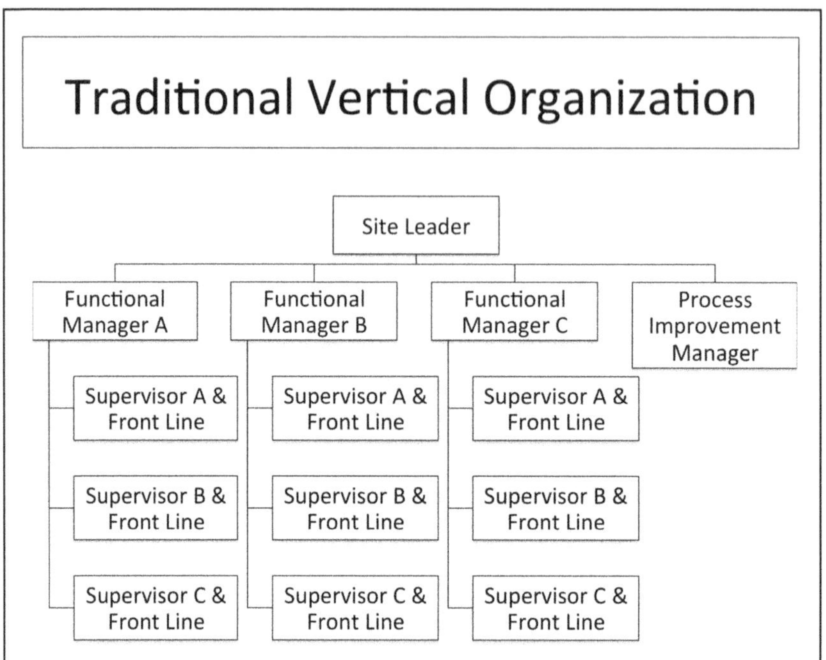

"Sara, what do you notice about the way this organization is laid out?"

"Nothing in particular. It looks pretty standard. It is certainly how our organization is structured. We even have a process engineer which is very similar to what you are showing in the chart."

"Ok, let's look a little bit closer and see what is actually going on in the organization."

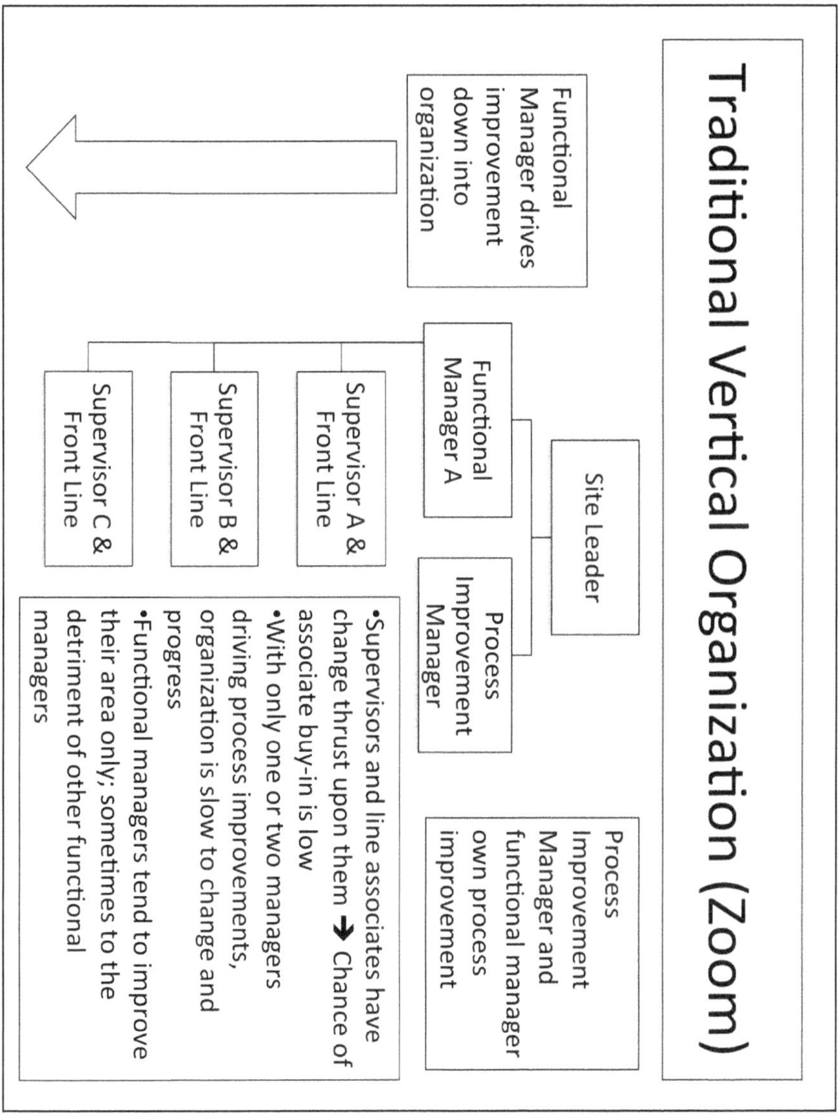

Traditional Vertical Organization (Zoom)

Site Leader

Functional Manager A

Process Improvement Manager

Supervisor A & Front Line

Supervisor B & Front Line

Supervisor C & Front Line

Functional Manager drives improvement down into organization

Process Improvement Manager and functional manager own process improvement

- Supervisors and line associates have change thrust upon them → Chance of associate buy-in is low
- With only one or two managers driving process improvements, organization is slow to change and progress
- Functional managers tend to improve their area only; sometimes to the detriment of other functional managers

"So, let's look at leg A of the organization. Typically what will take place in an organization like this is the site leader will dispense goals throughout the organization and A will be assigned two or three specific goals that may or may not slightly overlap with leg B's goals. A will make plans for a few step-change improvements. Some of these plans will negatively affect the other legs and a giant impasse is created."

Sara looked a bit puzzled. "Yes that makes sense, but doesn't it have to happen that way?"

"On paper it looks feasible, but, when you map the entire organization out, something else happens.

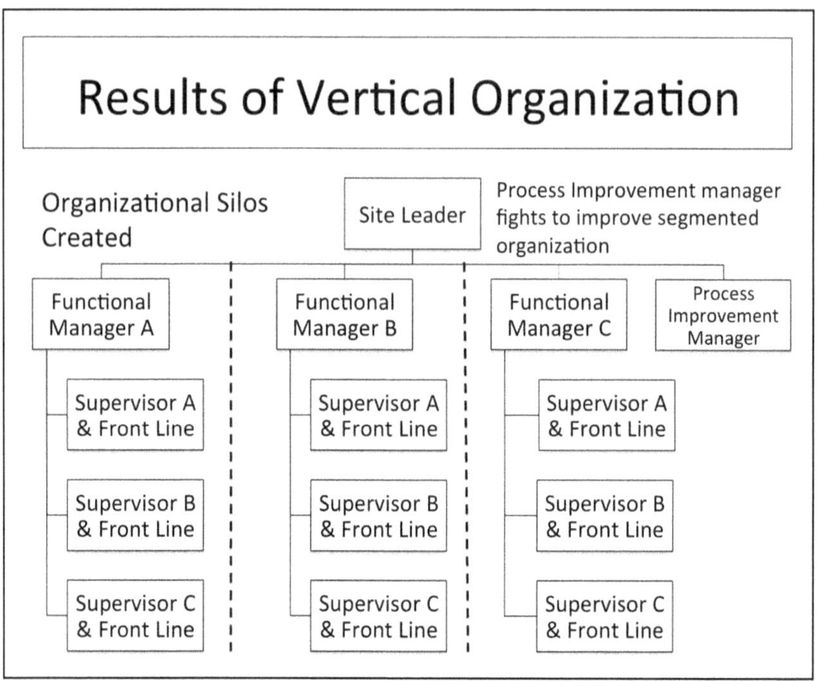

"The larger initiatives created by the functional managers adversely affect other departments. This sets up silos in the organization. This can also occur above the site level. It is very feasible that this could happen between executives. You could replace the title in the Site Leader box with CEO and replace the Functional Manager Box with Vice President. Mentalities like this have destroyed large companies."

"I guess that makes sense, but what is the other option? What is the alternative?"

I pulled up another generic organization chart.

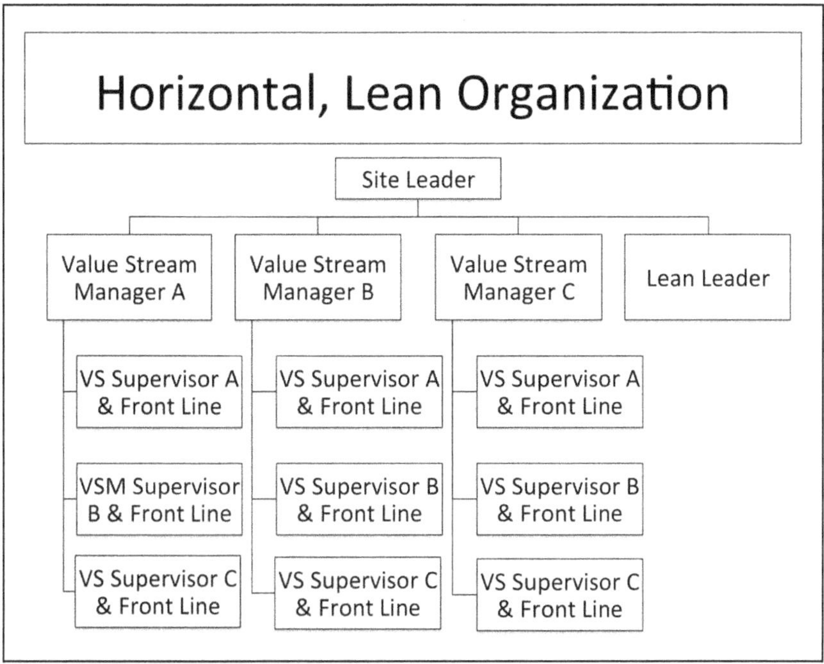

Sara busted out before I had a chance to start talking. "That looks exactly the same as the other one!"

"If you look at it in traditional terms, it is absolutely the same. Again, you have to take a closer look."

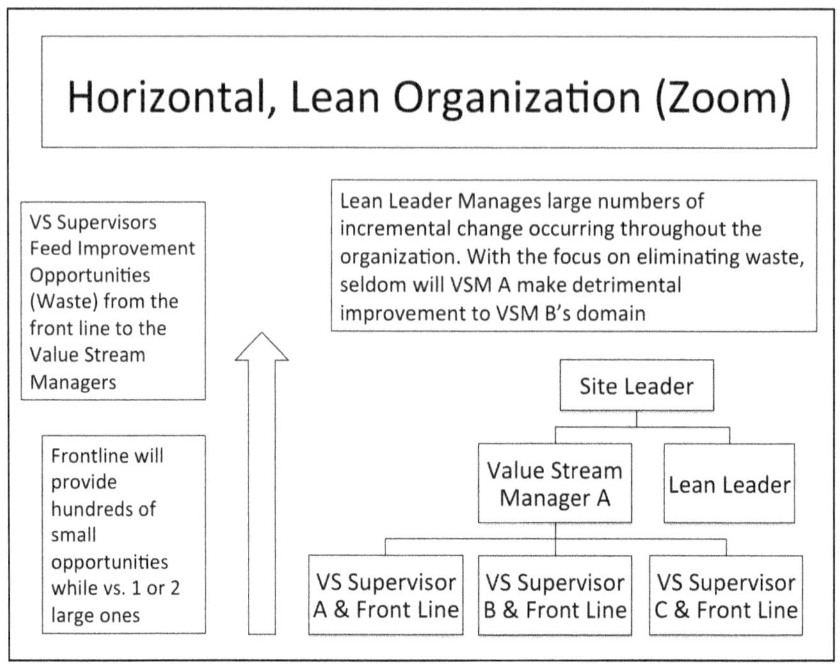

"So we have zoomed in on one leg of the organization. The difference is who is driving the improvements. The ideas come directly from the shop floor and involve eliminating waste that the front-line team finds as they are working. The supervisors and functional managers simply support their team. Change management becomes easy because, when you have the front-line team generating the ideas, you don't have to sell your thought process to them. Occasionally you will get to an impasse, but the lean leader and site leader can help navigate through those types of situations."

"It all seems confusing to me. You have to put a lot of trust in your team."

"Absolutely you do! This is the absolute opposite of micromanagement. Managers that require control will not thrive in this type of organization."

Sara waited again before speaking. "The overall organization chart looks the same, though."

"This mentality hasn't really caught up to Human Resources as of yet. This is how the org chart should really be drawn."

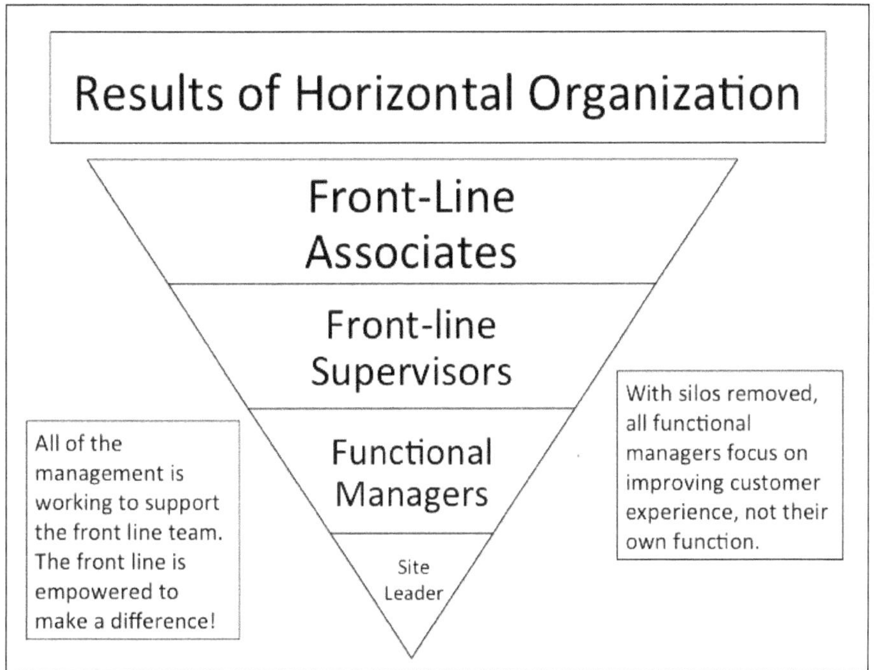

"The organization chart becomes inverted by practice. Since the front-line associates are performing the value-added work and generating the improvements, everyone else's only mission is to support them."

Sara looked frustrated again. "I guess that makes sense. Honestly, I just thought that at my stage in my career people would be supporting me."

"It is certainly admirable to be able to admit that, but I am certainly not writing your check to be supported. The safety department's role in any plant should be to support operations. We have a unique opportunity here to change the status quo company-wide. With your help we can reduce injuries and show the other plants how you and your department being a part of our lean journey helps make us safer and more productive. Many managers think that safety and production are at odds with one another. This could not be farther from the truth; in fact, they are interdependent! If we have a messy, unorganized workplace then people will make mistakes and get hurt. When we design a work place for flow, we become safer and more productive."

"So what do I do now? The team is very upset with me for calling Devon."

"It is going to be tough for you, at least for a little while. I would get on the floor and get involved. You took the right first step by admitting your mistake to the group. Get into motion and help support the front-line team. Also, support the management as well. We are going to need your help; the safety record here is abysmal and must get better. Once you start acting as a resource, magical things will happen. Come to the plant meeting in about fifteen minutes. As hard as this is going to be, the last thing you want to do is hide out in your office."

Sara still looked concerned as she left my office. I wondered if she was going to be able to make the transition from serve-me to service mentality.

There was about two weeks left until the first kaizen event and I was getting more and more antsy by the day. The "check-the-box" lean system at my last company was hardly an example of "good kaizen." The event was going to cost us thousands of dollars in overtime, reduced production, and supplies; my cost-conscious manager would absolutely look at the event as a negative unless we produced a seriously positive productivity increase.

17. SOME MUD IS STARTING TO STICK

As I was putting on my hard hat and safety goggles, it came to my attention that I had developed a new set of daily rituals. Before the move out here, my day was much more simple. I would hit the snooze button on my alarm; sometimes I would do this five times. I would go eat breakfast and charge through my day as fast as possible. Now I had a new timeline. My alarm only rang three times a week, because some of the time I would wake up naturally. During the times that it actually did hear it go off, I would never snooze. When I got to the plant, I would make my morning gemba walk. Usually, I would notice one or two other managers on the floor.

I hadn't previously realized it, but I never even found another psychiatrist after the big move. The team here was having just as big of an effect on me as I was on them. If I hadn't been making changes for the better, you can believe that Nichole would have let me hear about it. I certainly wasn't spending any less time at work over the last few months.

I proceeded out to the floor and noticed operators Dave and Mark looking at a hose connection to one of the reactor cleaning machines.

"What's going on?"

Mark started in. "I have been tripping over this thing for about a year and a half now."

Dave chuckled and responded, "Yeah, he definitely has. It is not hard to do when you wear size fourteen boots. I don't think your body ever grew into those feet."

"So we know this is a problem," I said. "What can we do about it?"

Mark asked, "Is there a way we can hard pipe the lines overhead? I suggested that when I first got here, but I was told no one would pay for it."

"Why don't you guys come off the floor for a bit with me? We need to set something up that I have been meaning to for a while, but I just haven't had the time. Meet me in the conference room. I need you to see if you can round up some white boards and some colored tape."

About fifteen minutes later I entered the conference room and not only were Dave and Mark there, but George and Johnny as well.

George seemed a bit nervous when he said, "What is going on? Why are Dave and Mark off the floor?"

"Whoa! No one is in trouble. It is time for us to set up a visual associate suggestion system. Mark has been tripping over the same piece of hose for over a year and no one has done anything about it. We need a way for the team to communicate up to the management."

George seemed relieved, but got a little bit defensive. "You know we have all been very busy and there is no easy fix for that."

"George, I don't know what an appropriate amount of time to fix a trip hazard is, but it is certainly less than eighteen months. We don't want to assign blame. What we want to do is create a way to visually track exposed problems."

Dave asked, "Why do we want to track them visually? Isn't it easier just to tell the manager?"

"How effective has it been for you guys to tell the manager? It doesn't look like it has. When you just tell the manager, what you are doing is removing the accountability from yourself and transferring it to them. We don't want that. We want the entire team to be identifying problems and helping with their solutions. By tracking it visually and supplying a potential corrective action you are holding the manager and yourselves accountable. We are all on the same team. Does that make sense?"

George seemed to relax a bit. "So what does the endgame look like here?"

"You guys make a list of whatever way best divides the facility and areas of responsibility up and I will be right back. Oh, and go get Steve; this is going to end up affecting him as well."

I came back to the room and, much to my surprise, there was much discussion. Steve seemed to be debating whether or not he should break logistics up into picking, receiving, material handling, and loading. George was discussing with Johnny whether or not the resin process should be subdivided into three parts. Dave and Mark were sitting down just watching the chaos unfold.

"Whoa. What's going on? This should be simple, not a yelling contest."

Steve exclaimed, "We have to plan this right up front or we will end up not having enough space to accommodate all of the ideas we will get."

It finally clicked in my head what the sensei was trying to teach me when he said that American engineers spend too much time in the design phase. It would literally take about ten minutes to make an extra logistics or production white board for suggestions, but the team was so worried about getting it right the first time that the analysis truly was crippling them.

"Look. Let's start simple. We aren't going to get ten thousand suggestions overnight. If it comes to a point that we need to break the process paths down even further, we will. We will let the team dictate that."

We finally settled on the following initial break down with resin broken up to be able to assign the other production supervisors to some of the areas on the list:

Plant Process Paths

- ❑ Resin production
  - – Main reactor
  - – Secondary reactors
  - – Packaging
- ❑ Solvent adhesive production
- ❑ Logistics

Next we needed to mock up one of the white boards for showing the progression of ideas from beginning to completion.

The team spent a few minutes discussing the format and we finally settled on the following:

Logistics Kaizen Tracking

New Ideas	Selected	In Progress	Completed

Mark asked, "So the basic concept is that we will submit suggestions for process improvements to our managers and they will be use this board to track the selection and completion?"

"Well, that is true, but there is more to it than that. Lean and kaizen are not just management responsibilities. They are the responsibility of the entire plant. Most of the kaizen ideas will come from sharp people like you and Dave, but the best results will come with you submitting an idea, working with your supervisor to fine-tune the idea, and implementing and standardizing the improvement together."

I handed out the blank CulturalKaizen™ Card to the team.

CulturalKaizen™ Card	
Date:	Name:
Area Waste Exists:	Type of Waste:
Describe the Waste:	
Potential Countermeasure:	

"So everyone has a card. Take a minute or so to fill out the card with a potential improvement idea and we will discuss them."

After a few minutes, Mark and Dave submitted the following to the team:

<table>
<tr><th colspan="2">CulturalKaizen™ Card</th></tr>
<tr><td>Date: 2/xx/xx</td><td>Name: Dave and Mark</td></tr>
<tr><td>Area Waste Exists: Main PVC Reactor Cleaning System</td><td>Type of Waste: Motion Waste (Safety Hazard)</td></tr>
<tr><td colspan="2">Describe the Waste: The flexible hoses that deliver solvent to clean the reactors after a product change are a trip hazard</td></tr>
<tr><td colspan="2">Potential Countermeasure: Replace the hoses with hard pipe that is routed overhead to remove the trip hazard</td></tr>
</table>

"Alright, so Mark has been exposed to a trip hazard for a good while now. Why don't you draw a sketch of the hazard and how the proposed solution will look on the white board?"

We spent about the next thirty minutes discussing the change and how the white boards would let us document and monitor the changes. By the end of the discussion, both Mark and Dave had taken greater ownership of their own area and continuous improvement as a whole.

Dave said, "We are going to get all of these boards posted so we can start documenting these ideas. Everyone out there has great ideas; we just don't have an outlet for all of them."

"We have Kaizen Cards - we should call the improvement area Kaizen Corner," Mark suggested.

Johnny said, "That's great, guys. If you keep putting in good ideas like this, we will make them happen. I honestly had no idea the trip hazard was an issue."

"One last thing, do you guys mind giving training to the rest of the team tomorrow? We want to solidify this as soon as possible. Also, I need you guys to help set the pace!"

I finally felt like we were getting some serious traction within the team. I had one final meeting with Johnny and George and then training with the kaizen team on Friday. On Monday, we were going all in.

18. PRE-KAIZEN JITTERS

Thursday Before Kaizen Week

I rolled by the gate at around early Thursday morning. I slipped Marcos a white paper bag and a cup of hot mochachino.

"What's in the bag, boss?"

"Muffins! One blueberry and one cranberry-cinnamon specially made for you. My wife likes to bake 'cause we can't get baked goods out here like we did back home. Enjoy!"

"Thanks. How are things going? Monday is the big day, huh?"

"Yes, it is. We have been preparing for this for months now. The team is ready. It's going to be a good thing."

"It has to be," Marcos said. "Everyone is a lot happier coming to work and I don't hear as many people complaining anymore. Can I ask you a silly question?"

"Anything. You have become like my personal shrink."

I hadn't seriously thought about it before, but in the absence of my psychiatrist, Marcos made a good stand in.

Marcos chuckled and asked, "Is it possible for everyone to be happy and the company to still make money?"

"If we are doing things right, we will have a happy workforce that is growing in numbers and we will make more and more money!"

"Wow! I hope you are right. Every boss we had before seemed to think that the more the employees complained, the more profitable we were."

The profoundness of that statement left me awestruck; however, thinking back to last July, I absolutely knew it was true. I remember being just as miserable and literally hating every minute of coming to work. It is an awful way to live and most of the world probably felt the same way at one point or another.

The only meeting I had scheduled for the day was a process check with Johnny and Steve regarding the kaizen event. I had read plenty of management books that encouraged me to focus on the vital few. I was hoping that I hadn't become a one-trick pony. I spent about 80% of the time talking about kaizen and lean tools to the team and the other 20% of the time I was planning talking about it.

Just about the time I was starting to daydream and contemplate the last several months of work, Johnny and George paged me from the conference room.

Before I sat down, I could tell that Johnny and George were a little bit tense. As usual, I was second guessing myself: had I been setting too high expectations? Was I setting them up to fail?

"What's going on guys? Are you ready for the big week, Johnny?"

George said, "That's what we wanted to talk to you about. I don't feel like we are ready to have the kaizen. There are still a lot of uncertainties. I don't know if the team will be ready. I think Johnny is solid, but the team is going to need more than the four hours of training you will be giving tomorrow."

Johnny added, "Look, I know all of the improvements we have done are successful, but I think we may have bitten off more than we can chew so soon!"

I took a few seconds before I responded. I wanted to think back to the feeling I had when I was running my kaizen with the sensei helping. I had expressed a similar concern to him.

"Sir, I just don't feel like we had enough preparation. We are totally unsure of the answer and we have had very little preparation time."

Speaking through his interpreter, the sensei said, "There would be no need for kaizen if you had the answer. You would have already solved the problem."

As I returned from my brief daydream, I tried to think of something similar to say to calm their nerves.

"Look, I feel like you guys are worried about failure. We have trained as a kaizen leader; we have implemented some lean tools on the floor; and we are training the team tomorrow. We are as prepared as we need to be. I know how you guys both feel right now; I certainly felt the same way. We just need to get in motion and we will figure out the details. One thing I can provide for you is a road map of the kaizen event."

I pulled up a slide from kaizen leader training onto the projector.

"This is the way I like to teach the format of the kaizen events initially. I want to keep it extra simple so people aren't scared. There are other improvement philosophies that are relatively complicated; my perception is that they turn off the front-line associate because they put too much emphasis on math and statistics. We will get more done by teaching fifty people a simple improvement system than by teaching three engineers a complicated improvement system. That said, at some point we have to add some details and more robust tools to the mix."

I clicked to the next slide.

Kaizen Roadmap: Day 1

Time	Monday
6:00	Intro, Agenda & Target Sheet/Opportunity
6:30	
7:00	Gemba Walk: Process Overview
7:30	
8:00	Map Out The Process & Identify Wastes
8:30	
9:00	
9:30	
10:00	
10:30	
11:00	Lunch
11:30	
12:00	Map Out The Process & Identify Wastes
12:30	
1:00	
1:30	
2:00	
2:30	
3:00	Action Plan & Report Out

Day 1 Milestones

- ❑ Gemba walk
- ❑ Team assignments for creating process map
- ❑ Begin creation of process map
- ❑ Begin identifying wastes
- ❑ Develop action plan for day 2
- ❑ Prepare report out from day 1

CULTURALKAIZEN

Almost instantaneously, Johnny looked a bit less anxious. A constant theme occurring within American manufacturing is that everyone wants a plan.

"There are several key items that must be accomplished on day one:

1. We must set the stage for a large step-change improvement. This is the time to reemphasize the target sheet and communicate the stretch goals to the team. We have to build a sense of urgency within the team; the large improvements we are targeting will put them in a state of mind that considers reinventing the process.
2. We need to perform a brief process walk. We did a great job at picking a cross-functional team; we have to introduce them to the area with a brief process overview. This should take no more than an hour.
3. We have to pick assignments for the team to map out the process. I will go over the individual assignments tomorrow during training. The main thing to remember is that we will have six people working together to map out an intensive and complicated process, instead of one or two people mapping out a simple process in training.

4. The mapping out of the process should begin after lunch on day one.
5. At the end of the day we need to develop an action plan for the next day and also prepare a short report of what happened during each day."

George looked intrigued and asked, "So that's all the team is responsible for on day one?"

"That's it. Kaizen and continuous improvement are simple processes. Improving something is simple conceptually. We don't need to spend time with highly cumbersome statistical tools. We need to find the waste and eliminate it. There is one thing that is absolutely paramount: the most important part of the kaizen is mapping out the process. If we do not get a quality process map, we will not be successful. It will take you through most or all of day two to document the process."

Johnny asked curiously, "We are going to spend over a hundred man-hours documenting the process? That seems like too many; what will take so long?"

"Excellent question. It will absolutely take that long to document every facet of the process. Most of the procedures created for the team are only looking at the meat of the process. They are looking at the value-added steps, such as initiating reaction and discharging product for packaging. What we need to eliminate is the white space in between those value-added steps. It will take significantly longer to document the forty minutes it took Aaron to locate a tool or Clarence attempting to pry the bolts off of the hatch that were stuck in place. All of these unnecessary tasks must be documented because they are where our opportunities lie."

"Do all those little bits of time really make that much of a difference? It doesn't seem like it would be significant." George questioned the concept.

"The key is the compounding of time. Saving five minutes here or there means nothing one time, but annualizing over a year makes small gains significant. What is the cycle time of the main reactor if you count discharge-to-discharge time? How many batches did we produce last year and what's the average revenue per batch?"

Johnny answered, "If we consider the main basis resin, about twelve hours to run the product and about 500 batches per year. I'm not familiar with the revenue. You had me get this data for the kaizen, remember?"

George added, "About eighty thousand per batch depending on the specialty additive package and medium it is packaged in. Could be as low as sixty or as high as one-forty."

"Great. Let's put some data up."

The Effects of Annualization	
Cycle time (hours)	12
Batches per year	500
Effect of 5 minute reduction (extra batches per year)	3.47
Average revenue per batch	$80,000
Total revenue increase	$277,600

Johnny and George's eyes were as wide as they could possibly be.

Johnny said, "So a five minute reduction in cycle time is worth over a quarter of a million dollars? That seems unbelievable."

Lean Learnings: The significance of the small improvements suggested from the front-line team is only evident when we take a step back and think!

"Based on the conditions we are in right now, it is absolutely accurate. In our current state, the plant is the constraint. We have a thirty-day backlog on orders. What we need to do is shift the constraint from the plant to the marketplace. We need to build excess capacity into the plant so that we are not always in scramble mode for production."

George nervously asked a question. "So if we have too much excess capacity, won't people be standing around with nothing to do?"

"In normal circumstances yes, but that is a good thing."

George said, "How is that a good thing? We would be paying them for nothing."

Johnny chimed in. "No! I get it. We would be paying them to continue to improve the process. George, do you realize how many daily kaizen projects we could get done with excess capacity?"

"Exactly! When we switch our mindset from making the project to improving the process, we unlock a world of possibilities."

George quipped, "Ok, I understand. What does day two of the kaizen look like?"

I went along to my next slide.

Kaizen Roadmap: Day 2

<table>
<tr><th>Time</th><th>Tuesday</th></tr>
<tr><td>6:00</td><td>Review Action Plan</td></tr>
<tr><td>6:30</td><td rowspan="9">Map Out The Process & Identify Wastes</td></tr>
<tr><td>7:00</td></tr>
<tr><td>7:30</td></tr>
<tr><td>8:00</td></tr>
<tr><td>8:30</td></tr>
<tr><td>9:00</td></tr>
<tr><td>9:30</td></tr>
<tr><td>10:00</td></tr>
<tr><td>10:30</td></tr>
<tr><td>11:00</td><td rowspan="2">Lunch</td></tr>
<tr><td>11:30</td></tr>
<tr><td>12:00</td><td rowspan="6">Identify & Trystorm Countermeasures to Identified Wastes</td></tr>
<tr><td>12:30</td></tr>
<tr><td>1:00</td></tr>
<tr><td>1:30</td></tr>
<tr><td>2:00</td></tr>
<tr><td>2:30</td></tr>
<tr><td>3:00</td><td>Action Plan & Report Out</td></tr>
</table>

Day 2 Milestones

- ❑ Complete process map
- ❑ Complete waste identification
- ❑ Begin identifying countermeasures to discovered wastes and try-storming solutions
- ❑ Develop action plan for day 3
- ❑ Prepare report out from day 2

CULTURALKAIZEN

"Day two also has some key items:

1. The complete process map should be finished on day two.
2. We should have a list of wastes identified by analyzing information used in creating the process map and the map itself.
3. We should start identifying some countermeasures for the wastes if possible.
4. Again, we need an action plan for day three and a report out from day two."

"How rigid are these guidelines?" asked Johnny.

"Not especially rigid; however, there are a few things that you will want to keep in mind. You want to err on the side of spending too much time mapping out the process. If you don't finish until the end of day two, it is totally appropriate. Just remember the roadmaps are a guide, not a class-schedule."

Day three was next:

Kaizen Roadmap: Day 3

Time	Wednesday
6:00	Review Action Plan
6:30	Trystorm Solutions
7:00	
7:30	
8:00	
8:30	
9:00	
9:30	
10:00	
10:30	
11:00	Lunch
11:30	
12:00	Trystorm Solutions
12:30	
1:00	
1:30	
2:00	
2:30	
3:00	Action Plan & Report Out

Day 3 Milestones

- ❑ Identify countermeasures to discovered wastes and try-storm solutions
- ❑ Develop action plan for day 4
- ❑ Prepare report out from day 3

CULTURALKAIZEN

"Day three is the meat of the process improvement. Provided that the process map is complete, all of day three should be dedicated to using the process map to identify wastes and trial countermeasures. The important thing to remember is that we must be on the floor 90% of the time try-storming the potential solutions."

"You have said that word 'try-storming' quite a bit. What exactly do you mean?" Johnny asked.

"To put it simply, try-storming is where brainstorming and execution collide. Try-storming is the middle ground between over-analyzing and preemptively executing. Try-storming is taking the right amount of data to make a decision. Many managers get stuck in the analysis-paralysis phase and can never recover. Other managers shoot from the hip constantly and never use facts to make decisions. The point is to use a process map to identify the wastes and use that knowledge to implement countermeasures. It doesn't take three weeks of data collection to be properly prepared and, by the same token, we also shouldn't rush into anything."

Kaizen Roadmap: Day 4

Time	Thrusday
6:00	Review Action Plan
6:30	Trystorm Solutions
7:00	
7:30	
8:00	
8:30	
9:00	
9:30	
10:00	
10:30	
11:00	Lunch
11:30	
12:00	Develop Plan for Implementation and Standardization
12:30	
1:00	
1:30	
2:00	
2:30	
3:00	Action Plan & Report Out

Day 4 Milestones

- ❑ Complete Try-storming process
- ❑ Begin developing a plan for implementation and standardization of the changes generated from the kaizen
- ❑ Develop action plan for day 5
- ❑ Prepare report out from day 4

CULTURALKAIZEN

"During day four, the team should be completing the bulk of the try-storming process. Additionally, in a plant like this, there could be some mechanical changes associated with the kaizen. We need to develop an action item list associated with knocking out the physical changes within thirty days. The changes need to be completed quickly or we will lose the momentum we create during the kaizen."

Kaizen Roadmap: Day 5

Time	Friday
6:00	Review Action Plan
6:30	Complete Standardization & Implementation Plan
7:00	
7:30	
8:00	Roll-out Results
8:30	
9:00	
9:30	
10:00	
10:30	Celebrate
11:00	
11:30	
12:00	
12:30	
1:00	OFF
1:30	
2:00	
2:30	
3:00	

Day 5 Milestones

- ❑ Roll-out Results of kaizen event
- ❑ Celebrate success with the team

"Day five is basically wrapping up the event. We should make presentations of our changes and findings to the entire organization. Also, we should celebrate the success of the event with the team."

George asked, "What do you mean celebrate?"

"We should have a big lunch at the end of the day. We should take the entire team out to a formal lunch at a nice restaurant."

George looked shocked at the prospect. "You can't do that - Devon is going to eat you for breakfast. You can't spend three or four hundred dollars on a dinner. It will blow the budget apart."

"I will just beg for forgiveness again. We have to do the right thing. Three hundred dollars won't blow the budget. We have to celebrate the kaizen. A kaizen is basically one giant team-building exercise. Edifying the successes will only help us grow the team and accelerate the transformation of the site. That's pretty much it. Are you guys ready for the training tomorrow?"

Leadership Learnings: "Do the right thing. It will gratify some people and astonish the rest."

–Mark Twain

Johnny said, “Yeah, the buzz of the kaizen has started to grow around the plant. I think this will be just what we need to help the plant grow.”

“I still can’t get over the fact that you will be taking the entire team out to sit-down lunch.” George was still stuck on the budget.

“Everything will be ok. The throughput gains will more than justify a little bit of food.”

“I hope so, but either way it will be fun to watch the fireworks.”

19. TRAINING DAY

Friday Before Kaizen Week

At the end of the Friday before kaizen week we had all six participants in the conference room for some pre-event training. I liked to use this opportunity for a few reasons. Firstly, it was a good chance to start and build some unity; secondly, it afforded me the opportunity to edify the kaizen team leader.

Team unity is absolutely paramount to success during a kaizen. I thought back to my first kaizen and the terrible struggle I faced while having to build unity during the kaizen. We hadn't been in the productive stage of the team until the end of day two and by that point it was a significant challenge in getting the team back on track.

It was about 2:00 pm and the team was starting to gather in the room. About five minutes past the hour I proceeded to start.

First Kaizen Event Team Training

1. Johnny- **Team Lead**
2. Enrique- Lab Tech **Co-Lead**
3. Dave- 1st shift Main Reactor Operator
4. Daniel O- 2nd Shift Solvent Operator
5. Trevor-1st Shift Warehouse Operator
6. Scott M- 2nd Shift Maintenance Tech

We are in the business of improving our manufacturing and distribution processes!

"Team, the six of you are about to start something very significant. You are members of the inaugural kaizen team. By the same token, this will carry a substantial amount of responsibility and accountability. I tend to be an exceptionally positive and upbeat person when talking to the whole team, but this kaizen team was hand-selected for a reason. I would be doing you a disservice if I sugarcoated the business realities."

Dave spoke up, "What is the business situation? How can the six of us help?"

"Dave, the plastic business here is broken. Our customers' expectations are never met. We promise ten and fifteen day lead times. We almost never hit those numbers. We make a significant amount of off-spec product that has to be shipped out as hazardous waste. That's the bad news. The good news is that you all can fix it!"

Daniel spoke up. "I hate to repeat the question, but seriously: how can the six of us save the company? We are all only high school educated. And I might not be a high school drop-out, but they certainly wanted me gone from there as fast as possible!"

It suddenly hit me. These guys were all victims of bad programming. It may have been how they grew up or the previous managers here, but I hadn't previously realized the ubiquitous self-esteem battle I was fighting in addition to a process battle.

"Daniel, I totally get where you are coming from. I don't want to sound like a broken record; however, the key to our success will be your intimate knowledge of the process. Senior managers fly around at 30,000 feet. They get the high points only. You and the rest of the team are down in the trenches every single day. You know the processes inside and out!"

Scott, the maintenance technician, chimed in. "Yes, but the only operator from the main reactor on the team is Dave. I don't mean to be rude, but you seem to be contradicting yourself, right?"

"Excellent observation, Scott! I don't *just* want intimate experience. Is there anyone here that thinks they know how to run the reactor better than Dave? Does anyone not think that Dave could basically do it blindfolded?

I waited for a few seconds and Trevor finally spoke up. "Dave has been doing it for so many years that he could regurgitate the fifty or sixty steps to you without looking at the procedure. He's the man! He trains every new operator and he never fails a batch."

Dave looked over at Trevor and quipped, "Aww, thanks buddy! I didn't know you cared."

Everyone chuckled.

"Ok, so we have established that Dave could be an expert witness during a trial. Would there be any value in having a duplicate of him on the team?"

"Not really. I think I figured it out!" said Enrique.

"Go ahead."

"You want a mix of experienced personnel and a fresh set of eyes who are willing to question the normal process. It will help the team think 'outside-the-box.'"

"Perfect! I couldn't have said it any better myself!"

Johnny said, "I think this would be a good time to show them the target sheet."

I pulled up the target sheet for the team.

Revised Kaizen Event Target Sheet

Event Description (work center) **Main Reactor Product A- 60% of volume**	Event Dates 2/12-2/16

	Current	Target	Day 1	Day 2	Day 3	Day 4	Final	% Δ
Cycle time	12	6						
Volume per day								
Space (sq. ft.)								
Inventory								
Walking distance								
Transport distance								
Changeover time (hours)	2	1						
Quality improvements								
Visual controls	0	2						
Safety improvements								

Dave said, "How in the world are we going to take the cycle time down six hours?"

Johnny started to take ownership of the team. He poked out his chest and responded, "That's why we are having the kaizen! We don't know how yet. We are going to spend about 250 man-hours mapping out every facet of the process and developing solutions. I know there is way to hit these numbers; we just have to put all of our heads together to figure it out!"

"Does anybody else feel like we are about to go win the next big game?" Daniel responded.

Everyone laughed.

Johnny got a little bit defensive and said, "You guys know how many plants they have closed down and also how many have mysteriously appeared overseas. We have a chance here to make a difference!"

"He is right. If we can pull this off, I can absolutely see some of the first kaizen leaders and team members being flown all over the country to work with other plants; however, we have to make our own bed first!"

I pulled up the first slide.

Week-long Kaizen Event

- ❑ Take a picture of the process to spot the waste
- ❑ Try-storm countermeasures to remove the waste
- ❑ Put Systems in place to sustain the countermeasures

"You guys remember the basic kaizen steps, right? Well, now it's time to actually go a bit deeper into the process."

Dave said, "It's about time. I feel like that kaizen is some kind of secret society."

Enrique, who I would later learn was more than a little bit competitive, said, "Yes and we all made the team!"

"It's certainly not like a 'Skull and Bones' group, but we do want to keep a certain amount of mystique to kaizen. Kaizen is special and members of the team are special as well."

Time to get back to business.

"So, when I use the phrase take a picture of the process, what does that mean to you all?"

Trevor said, "I think it means you want us to investigate the process."

"Basically, I want you all to compile different kinds of information about how our current process works."

"Don't all of you production guys have procedures for making product? Isn't that already mapped out?" Scott asked.

Just as I was about to say something, Dave beat me to it. "We do, somewhat, but they aren't accurate and they certainly don't cover everything that is going on between the time we charge the reactor to the time we discharge it."

"Exactly. The picture we want to take is a very detailed picture. It is going to take the team the first two days of the kaizen just to take the picture."

Trevor exclaimed, "Wow, that is a serious picture!"

"Developing the process map is the most important part of the event. It's so important that each of you will have specific tactical jobs. This will prevent people from duplicating work during the event. The first job we need to assign is process pilot. The process pilot will serve as our tour guide through the main reaction area. We need someone who knows the main reactor like the back of his or her hand. It has to be someone who can easily guide us through the proper sequence of activities. Who do you all think should be our process pilot?"

Enrique said, "That's easy. It has to be Dave."

Johnny and I gave each other a nod. It was obvious the team was starting to come together.

Process Mapping Assignments

Role	Purpose	Person Assigned
Process Pilot	Someone intimately familiar with the process who can lead the team on the walk	Dave

"Great! Next we need a scribe. The scribe is responsible for accurately recording each action of the process on a process map log. This is the document we will use to build our process map from. The scribe is an important job. They have to be very accurate because they will be capturing all the steps of the process including:

- A detailed overview of each process step.

- The time required for each step.
- Who is performing each task.
- The inventory accruing at each step."

Daniel said, "Enrique is the one who should be doing this. He has to do all that ISO paperwork we are required to do to ship to the aerospace industry."

Process Mapping Assignments

Role	Purpose	Person Assigned
Process Pilot	Someone intimately familiar with the process who can lead the team on the walk	Dave
Scribe	Documents the sequence of activities	Enrique

"Alright, two down. The next job is the surveyor. The surveyor builds a spaghetti diagram of the process in conjunction with the scribe's documentation."

Johnny sounded a bit exasperated and asked, "What in the world is a spaghetti diagram? That is definitely a new one for me."

The rest of the team laughed. Johnny wasn't the kind of guy to show weakness unless he had to.

"Let me show you one; that will be easier than trying to explain it."

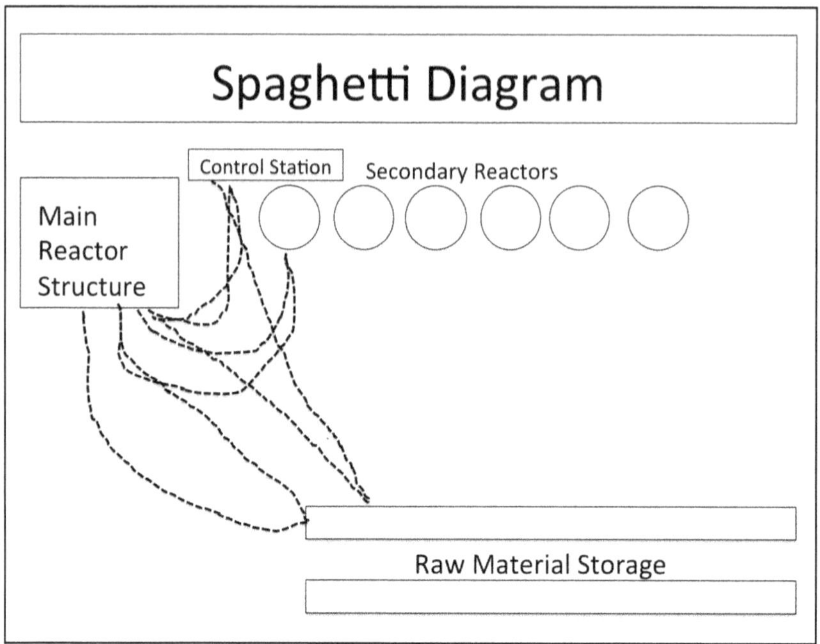

"So this one is a little bit crude, but it gets the point across. Basically, the point is to map out the flow of people, information, and materials visually. We will synchronize the spaghetti diagram with the steps of the process recorded by the scribe. We should label each of the three flows. This will help us see where the waste is. The goal is to have less spaghetti noodles on the plate when we are finished than when we started."

Trevor laughed. "We have all kinds of crazy new words, but spaghetti diagram definitely is the funniest."

"Does anyone have any objections to having Trevor being our surveyor?"

Process Mapping Assignments

Role	Purpose	Person Assigned
Process Pilot	Someone intimately familiar with the process who can lead the team on the walk	Dave
Scribe	Documents the sequence of activities	Enrique
Surveyor	Prepares the spaghetti diagram that shows the flow of people, materials & information	Trevor

"Two more jobs left. Next up is the navigator. The navigator's job is to pace for the surveyor. The navigator helps measure the distance between all the steps of the process. The navigator will account for the distance that people, information, and materials travel through the process. This will help the kaizen team focus their efforts on eliminating the tasks that are causing the most detriment to the process."

Johnny replied, "Let me take that step."

Process Mapping Assignments		
Role	Purpose	Person Assigned
Process Pilot	Someone intimately familiar with the process who can lead the team on the walk	Dave
Scribe	Documents the sequence of activities	Enrique
Surveyor	Prepares the spaghetti diagram that shows the flow of people, materials & information	Trevor
Navigator	Calculates the distance between each step and informs the surveyor	Johnny

"Alright, that sounds good. The last step in the process is the spotter. Daniel and Scott will make excellent spotters. We want people that are foreign to the process using the process walk as a way to identify waste. They will record the waste on a Waste Log. This doesn't mean that everyone else will ignore waste that they see; Daniel and Scott will be the primary personnel accountable for it. I would think that in a process this size you would be able to find no less than twenty separate wastes on the floor. Be prepared to log what kind of waste you are capturing. It is also important for one of you to bring a camera to digitally document the waste. It will make it easier to reference while the team is assembling the process map out of all of those sticky notes."

Process Mapping Assignments		
Role	Purpose	Person Assigned
Process Pilot	Someone intimately familiar with the process who can lead the team on the walk	Dave
Scribe	Documents the sequence of activities	Enrique
Surveyor	Prepares the spaghetti diagram that shows the flow of people, materials & information	Trevor
Navigator	Calculates the distance between each step and informs the surveyor	Johnny
Spotter	Identifies sources of waste	Daniel & Scott

Enrique said, "So we have this giant to-do list for the process map; what do we do once we find all of the waste?"

"It's not as simple as what do we do. Once the map is built, you have to listen to it. It will almost talk to you. There are a few things you can look for specifically:

1. Workarounds: are there people in the process who have invented their own off-line way of going around a problem? If so, solve the problem.
2. Are there any choke points on the process map? Choke points can be especially bad. Are there two lines feeding one output? If so, can you relieve this burden through scheduling or diversion?
3. It depends: if you ask an associate any question and the response is 'it depends', you generally have an opportunity. What the statement 'it depends' really means is: "We do not have any process for this whatsoever!" All you have to do in this situation is define the process.
4. Next you want to label all the tasks in the process map 'value-added,' 'non-value added,' or 'non-value added but necessary.' If you have more than 30% value-added steps, you probably do

not have a detailed enough process map. You should regroup and fill in the details of the process map. Anything that is not truly 'value-added' is up for grabs. You can eliminate a great deal of steps. Remember: purpose first, process second!

5. You should look and see the connections between the 'value-added' steps and be able to determine:
    a. Is there a connection delay?
    b. How often does a connection get delayed?
    c. Is there standard work for the connection?
    d. Who makes the connection?
    e. Can the connection be eliminated?
    f. Is the connection clear (are responsibilities defined)?
6. Is there a way to simplify activities?
7. Is there a way to combine activities?
8. Can you rearrange activities to prevent handoffs?"

Enrique responded, "Your answer was too long!"

Everyone laughed. It was about time to wrap up training. Although I was a bit embarrassed, I was glad that he broke the tension.

"There are basic tools you guys can use from the Toyota system, but I don't want to put ideas in your head right now. Finding the waste is the important part. If you have found the waste and you are lost for an answer, I will help. Generally, that is not the case. Once you find the waste, the answer will present itself. Does anyone have any questions?"

"What are we going to eat next week?" Trevor replied.

"I am going to cater the event from a few different places and we are going out on Friday afternoon; why?"

I asked why but I knew why. These guys had never been respected on basically any level. It wasn't the management team left onsite; it was the previous senior leadership and the plant manager that had left a bad taste in their mouths.

The room was silent.

"Don't worry. You all will eat well. Try and get some sleep before next week. We are going to be extra busy!"

20. GETTING THE KAIZEN TEAM IN GEAR

I could hardly sleep Sunday night before the first kaizen event. This was going to be a big week for us. We had done a significant amount of planning, training, and supporting the team.

Nichole rolled over to me and said, "Everything is going to be ok. You guys have done everything that you could possibly do to make this week successful."

"I know, but the self-doubt is starting to creep in. I haven't had years of exposure to this problem-solving philosophy. In actuality, what I have had is a bad example of its implementation. I have used that as a model for what *not* to do. I really like it here and I like watching the team grow. I feel like we can do a great deal of good; I want the business to be successful."

She smiled and said, "You may as well go ahead into work. You aren't going to get any more sleep tonight and you are keeping me awake."

"You are right. I will go ahead in."

As I was walking out of the bedroom door she looked up at me and asked, "Are you still sad?"

I hadn't really thought about it; I had spent too much time focusing on other people to be concerned with myself. It was almost like my problems miraculously disappeared.

Leadership Learning: People are only happy when they are in the pursuit of a worthwhile goal. That goal may or may not line up with your business goals. Embrace them either way.

I passed through the gate to the plant at about 4:00 am.

Marcos said, "Today is the big day; right, sir?"

"It is a big day for the team and the plant. I'm just trying to set them up for success."

"I saw Johnny drive through the gate about an hour ago. He seemed pretty anxious himself. I asked him how he was doing and he said nervous. I think this is a big step for him."

"It is. He is going to be fine. Johnny is a driven, smart supervisor with a lot to be proud of. This is a new experience for him. Just like all other new experiences, it is going to take some getting used to."

Marcos shook his head and said, "I hope it works out for us. Keep me posted please."

"No problem! I'm sure that the team will keep you up to date, though."

I walked out onto the shop floor and I saw that Johnny was setting up a table for the team. He had packs and packs of yellow, green, red, and blue stickies. Two flip charts were stationed out on the floor and he had printed two 24" x 36" posters. One of the posters was the target sheet and one of them was a list of the seven wastes.

"You look ready to go!"

"I am," Johnny said. "We are going to do everything we can to hit you a home run!"

"You don't need to do it for me. Do it for the plant. Do it for the sake of these jobs."

Johnny smiled and said, "So how do we play this? What steps do we need to take today?"

"One thing we should do that I hadn't previously mentioned is let's have an opening meeting with the whole plant at 6:00 am. Talk to them about what the team will be working on and what you all hope to achieve. This will also give the team the opportunity to set the other associates at ease. There are going to be six team members taking detailed notes about what everyone is working on. It is easy to get nervous with that many people looking over your shoulder."

"Got it," Johnny responded. "What are you going to be doing? Will I be able to get in touch with you if I need you?"

"Absolutely!" I said. "I have cleared my calendar for the entire week. Just let me know if you need anything. I will be floating out on the floor. I'm not going to be bothering you guys; I want this to be your event. However, if you need some support, feel free to let me know."

At 6:00 am we all met in the break room. Johnny had the entire team stand up in front of the group. There were a few people that were disinterested, but much fewer than there were the first time I stood in front of the group. We were seeing the signs of change and this week would help us segue into a true culture of continuous improvement.

Johnny gave everyone a brief overview of what would be taking place over the next several days. There were a few questions and he or someone on his team answered them very intelligibly and was able to articulate on the purpose behind each step.

"Good job! Please make sure we do the same thing at 2:00 pm for the second shift crew."

"No problem," Enrique said.

The team made their way out to the shop floor, where Johnny had set up the kaizen area and started getting ready to perform their waste walk.

"Couple of things, real quick team. I need to go over some forms that will help you with your process map. Then it's all on the team. Who is the process pilot?"

Dave stepped up and said, "That's me!"

"Make sure you are going at a reasonable enough pace that your team will be able to keep up with you while completing their forms."

"That makes sense," Dave agreed.

"Which one of you will be serving as the scribe?"

Enrique spoke up, "I will. What do you have for me?"

I handed him a few of the following forms:

Process: ____________________ Name: ________________ Date: _______

Step #	Who is Performing?	What is being performed?	Box Time	Distance Traveled

CULTURALKAIZEN Process Map Log Page ___ of ___

"Enrique, as Dave is giving you a tour of the process, use these sheets to document what is happening. At the same time you should be receiving information from Johnny, our navigator, regarding the amount of distance between each process step. This distance can take the form of materials, people, information or, more likely, some combination of all three."

"I have a question," Enrique said. "What is box time?"

"Box time is simply the amount of time that each step takes. I refer to it as box time because it's the number that goes into the box of the yellow sticky when you guys are building your process map. Some people refer to it as step time or step cycle time. I would rather keep it simple. Simple things work the best and make more sense."

"Where is Trevor at?"

"Right here!" he replied.

"The next sheet is for you since you are our surveyor."

I handed him four of the following sheets:

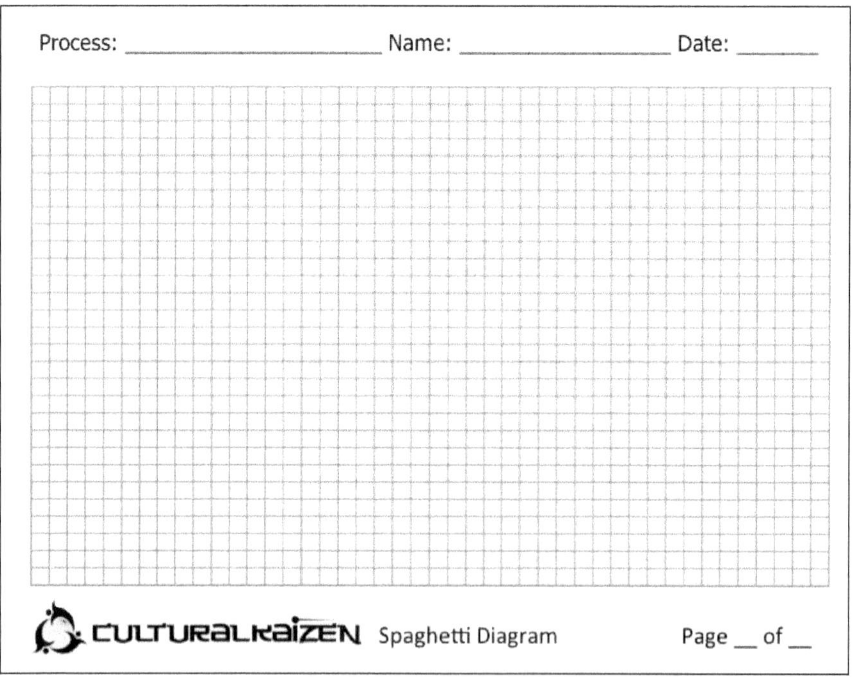
Process: ____________ Name: ____________ Date: ______

CULTURALKAIZEN Spaghetti Diagram Page __ of __

"Use this form to make the top-down map like we talked about last Friday. Make sure you are syncing up with Enrique. It will be helpful to draw numbers by each motion that correspond with the step numbers that he is logging on the process map log."

“I had purchasing pick up one of those wheels that indicates distance traveled,” Johnny chimed in. “We will make sure that the distances are extra accurate.”

“That’s great. Thank you!” I replied. “The last form is for Daniel and Scott.”

I handed them both three copies of the last form:

Process: ____________________ Name: ________________ Date: ______

Step #	Transportation	Inventory	Motion	Waiting	Over Production	Over Processing	Defects	Description of the Waste	Potential Countermeasures

CULTURALKAIZEN TIM WOOD Observation Log Page __ of __

“Both of you guys are going to be stalking Tim Wood. Use this form to make note the wastes you see in the process. Also, if you can quickly jot down a potential countermeasure, write it down. The important part is to note the wastes, not to focus on the countermeasures. Also, if anyone else notes wastes, make sure you record those as well. Everyone should have a part in waste identification.”

“Does anyone have any questions?”

“Nope,” Trevor said. “Let us get to work!’

“Nice!” I replied.

Johnny gave me a nod as they scurried off to begin mapping out the process. I thought about the time I was running my kaizen event in my previous role. The almost cryptic words of the sensei continued to echo in my ear. *"When you have a proper respect for people, they will go to the ends of the earth for you."*

I heard Dave off in the distance. "This is where we receive our manufacturing orders from Johnny…"

21. TAKING A PICTURE OF THE CURRENT STATE

Yet again, I looked down at my phone and saw the ominous caller ID screen:

Devon Carpenter
952-555-1212

The proximity of his call to day one of our kaizen event had me concerned. I thought back to one of my previous mentors telling me to take a deep cleansing breath.

"Good morning, Devon. How are you today?"

"I'm doing well, thank you. I just wanted to go over some of the numbers you sent to me for the plant KPIs."

"No problem. What questions do you have?"

I pulled up the listing he had provided to me and the report I sent to him; some additional items had been added since our last conversation.

Devon's Metrics

- ❑ No injuries
- ❑ Increase unit productivity 20%
- ❑ Cut manufacturing operating budget by 15%
- ❑ Increase customer satisfaction indicator from 60% to 90% (A^+ order)
- ❑ Direct labor reduction 10%
- ❑ Reduce waste disposal 10%
- ❑ Inventory accuracy 99%

Plant Metric Report

Metric	Target	Nov	Dec	Jan	To Date Feb
Injuries	0	0	0	0	0
Productivity Improvement	20%	-3%	0%	7%	9%
Budget Improvement	15%	-3%	0%	5%	7%
A^+ Order	90%	60%	58%	74%	72%
Direct Labor Reduction	10%	0%	0%	0%	0%
Waste Reduction	10%	3%	-5%	4%	4%
Inventory Accuracy	99%	68%	73%	81%	83%

"Can you tell me about the safety performance of the plant? Last year there were three significant injuries at the site and about seven minor ones.

How is it possible that you haven't had any injuries since you have been there?"

"We have had a big focus lately to have managers spending as much time as possible out on the shop floor working with the teams. We have spent a great deal of time focusing on correcting safety issues."

I could hear him typing on the other end of the phone. I was wondering if this discussion would be referenced in a later conversation.

"Tell me about your productivity result."

"We are not quite at the target yet, but we will get there."

"No, that's not what I mean. You are the second highest plant in terms of productivity improvements. What have you done to do this? Have you made any unauthorized capital improvements?"

"Oh my. Not at all. We have been spending time working on material flow. That's pretty much it. The operators were telling me that they were having a significant amount of waiting delay due to the time they had to wait for material to be delivered to their work center. The first-line supervisor helped the team put together a system to get rapid material deliveries."

"Hmm…ok."

He started typing again.

"What about the budget improvement? It sounds to me like you are spending more money, not cutting costs."

"Well, one of the biggest causes of 'out of specification' batches was the wrong raw material being transported to the job site. We have many less 'bad' batches now; therefore, we have to ship out less hazardous waste. Hazardous waste disposal is about twenty to thirty thousand per truck."

Again, he started typing relentlessly.

"Alright, thanks for the update. I will be in touch soon."

Though the conversation could have gone a lot better, it could have gone quite a bit worse as well. I proceeded to make my way out to the floor to touch base with the kaizen team. They had been going at it hard for about six hours now.

I arrived in the main reactor area with the entire team extremely engaged.

Dave was shouting over the large pump motors. "This is where we run the purge cycle between the batches. The operator controls the process from this control board along the north wall."

Enrique's process map log was about five pages deep at this point and the spaghetti diagram being prepared by Trevor was starting to be illegible due to the massive amounts of intersecting lines muddling the space.

I went over to peek at Scott and Daniel's Tim Wood Observation forms.

Process: Main Reactor Name: Scott & Daniel Date: 2/12

Step #	Transportation	Inventory	Motion	Waiting	Over Production	Over Processing	Defects	Description of the Waste	Potential Countermeasures
1				X				Waiting for material orders when none are ready	
11			X					Traveling up and down the stairs 18 times for loading the reactor	
X	X	X					X	Failed batches in drums clogging up floor space	
14	X		X					Small chemical addition (<10 lbs.) station located 100 paces from addition station	
15			X					Operator looking for tools to close reactor hatch	
36	X					X		Pumping Raw material to a holding tank before pumping to main reactor	
45	X	X			X			Sending Finished Base Material to a holding tank and waiting to process in secondary reactor	

CULTURALKAIZEN TIM WOOD Observation Log Page 1 of 3

Daniel asked quickly, "That's waste right?"

"What is?"

"Having to wait for material order forms to be generated prior to us preparing a batch."

"It can be waste. The waiting certainly is."

Scott stated, "Coming out here to watch these guys work has given me a new sense of respect for them. They are pushing all day long. It's eight hour days of long and hard work. The least we could do for them is provide a decent tool for closing the reactor. The wrench they need is less than $100. We should have one of these by every workstation."

"I agree. The last thing I want to be doing while I am working on a project at the house is going out to the garage to dig through my tool box. This is basically the same concept."

Enrique came over to our little huddle and gradually the entire team was standing around Scott and Daniel.

"There is another thing that is driving us crazy," Enrique said. "There is a significant amount of time spent pumping material back and forth between different holding tanks."

"Why is that occurring?"

Enrique looked puzzled and said, "What do you mean? Don't we need to just find the waste and stop it?"

"Well, not exactly. There could be a perfectly valid reason that the activity is taking place. We have to find out why the waste is occurring. Dave, why do you pump to these intermediate storage tanks instead of pumping directly to the smaller reactors?"

"It depends. We could have direction from management to stop producing that batch and to start producing another batch instead," Dave commented.

Johnny added his two cents. "We kind of listen to whichever customer is screaming at us the loudest. They pump to one of the holding tanks in case we need to break into the schedule. I will leave the material there for up to seventy two hours and then we will process the next batch in the main reactor."

"Why not just send it to the secondary reactor and then start a new batch in the main reactor?"

Johnny replied, "Well, it will take a few hours to get the secondary reactors going and we want to start the hot order as soon as possible. It could mean the difference of half of a day for the customer getting their shipments. Does that make sense?"

I thought about this for a little bit more and asked, "How many batches go through the holding tanks?"

Johnny responded, "Just the ones that make way for the hot orders."

I heard Trevor whisper, "Come on, Dave. Tell him."

Dave responded reluctantly, "That's not exactly true. We kind of pump every batch through the holding tanks, because the schedule is broken into so many times."

Johnny did not looked pleased.

Johnny asked, "How long have we been doing this for? What happened to change this?"

Dave responded, "About two or three years…well, the schedule as getting broken into so many times that it just seemed easier this way."

Lean Learning: At all levels, your team and their teams are self-optimizing; given enough time, they will do pretty much anything to make their jobs simpler. This is an asset, not a liability. Make the decision to standardize and capitalize on it!

I could see where this was going and I interjected quickly, "Team, remember. We aren't here to place blame or judgment. We are simply taking a picture of the process. Every one of you has pictures that don't look the best. We just want to capture those items and manage them. If they are required, we should try to optimize them. If they can be eliminated, let's make a plan to do so. Day one and two are fact finding only."

Johnny seemed to be diffused. "Alright, let's keep taking that picture. Excuse us, boss."

Everyone laughed.

I seemed to be becoming the target for a great deal of jokes. Anyone who has ever spent a significant amount of time in a plant knows that this is a good thing.

The process mapping portion of the kaizen was coming together nicely and additionally it seemed like the team was working well with each other. I decided that I did not want to interrupt the creative process any more so I headed up to my office to do some more of my non-value added administrative tasks.

Day One Report Out

At about 3:00 pm the team made their way up to the conference room to give their report out for the day.

"How did everyone make out?"

Enrique perked up. "We did well. We are about 50% finished with the process map. We have started to compile the information on a wall in the gemba. There are already about fifty yellow stickies up and we have barely put a dent in the process map log."

"Good. Johnny, let's walk through your day."

"No problem. Our day flowed like this:

1. We gave a brief to the plant about what we would be working on during this week.
2. We had a discussion regarding the target sheet and how we were going to attack our goals.
3. We used our previously designated assignments and started in our different roles for taking a picture of the process.
4. We identified some initial wastes and logged them into the Tim Wood observation form.
5. We started compiling all of the data and observations we gathered into the process map."

"Excellent. What is your plan for tomorrow?"

"Tomorrow we are going to complete the process map and we will begin analyzing it to focus our efforts so that we are targeting the parts of the process that will give us the most benefit."

"Good. Alright, it's question time. Dave, what did you learn today?"

Dave seemed to be caught a bit off guard by my question but responded, "I realized that I am an expert in the process. Your comments struck me as strange when you said that the operators know the unit. I got about five thousand questions today from the kaizen team and there was very little that I wasn't able to answer. Also, I learned that there is a huge amount of waste that we need to take care of. It was very eye-opening. I have worked here for sixteen years and I never took a step back to ask 'why' are we doing something."

"Good! Trevor, what about you? Did you pick up any useful information from today's work?"

Trevor responded, "I never realized how much time the operators spend waiting for different things. Just today we saw that they are waiting for:

1. The batch to come to temperature.
2. The low pressure steam system had to be brought on line along with the flare system.
3. The lab to finish first pass quality results so they can add the catalyst to the reactor.
4. The material handler to move the finished product if they are packaging into 2,000 pound bulk bags.
5. The operator was searching for a large wrench to close the man-way before starting the reactor. I guess the operator wasn't waiting, but the batch sure was. It took him about fifteen minutes to wait for another operator to finish up with their batch."

"Johnny, how much is five minutes worth to the company over a year?"

Johnny exclaimed, "Over $250,000."

The team looked astonished, but I moved along to the next team member anyway. "Scott, what about you?"

"I learned that what you have been telling us seems to be making a lot of sense. When you pull a team together to solve a problem it works out much better."

"Did you learn anything about the process?"

"Yes, we are sending raw material to a holding tank as well before charging it to the main reactor. That step seems unnecessary. Dave says we fill the holding tank with a pump and then gravity feeds it to the main reactor."

"That's strange. Why do we do it?"

"Well, the holding tank is on weigh cells so we can get an accurate weight. The flow meter on the pump was broken many moons ago and no one bothered to fix it. It has just become standard practice now to use the holding tank as a way of estimating how much material we are using. The pipe was even removed when they rerouted the pump."

"Wow. That seems like a big waste."

Johnny shook his head and said, "I didn't even know about that one. We need to get that meter fixed. That one thing could save us twenty minutes for each batch!"

"Good. Just make sure you keep looking for waste. We don't want to jump to conclusions yet. Just keep looking for as much waste as possible. Daniel, what did you find out today?"

"I couldn't believe that the operators were walking about 100 yards to the small chemical addition weigh station and then walking back to the main reactor to make the addition. In addition to being a production waste, carrying hazardous chemicals across the room is too much risk for us to undertake. We can't let this one fall off our plate. This is a huge safety win for us!"

Enrique chimed in. "I learned that the reactor operators have to be in shape; they climb up and down the mezzanine eighteen times for this particular product family."

"Wow. What are they up there doing?"

"There are five manual valves that have to be manipulated and then the operator has to go down to the control panel to start the raw material transfer. It is a very complicated process."

"Good. What about you, Johnny?"

"Well, I learned that I need to take a deep breath and just take a picture of the process. There are many problems here, but there are problems everywhere. We just need to get them out in the open and solve them."

"Very good. Has every one had a good day?"

Trevor continued his usual banter. "Yes, but we are tired. We need more food tomorrow!"

"I will see what I can do. Just stay engaged like you all are today. I promise we will eat good on Friday afternoon."

22. A PERFECT STORM OF STICKIES

I didn't make my way through the gate until about 7:30 am. This was a significant rarity for me. I had been awake until about 1:00 am last night working on a report for our financial operations department. In retrospect, it was not right for me to absorb so many administrative tasks, but my mentality at the time was to take as much off of my team so that they would catch the kaizen bug.

Marcos quipped, "There you are; I was getting worried about you. The kaizen team got here about 5:00 am. I think they wanted to get a head start on the day. Johnny mentioned something about not having enough time."

I faintly chuckled and said good-bye to Marcos. A kaizen event places very high expectations on the team leader. The team leader feels the weight of the entire plant on their shoulders, regardless of how many times you tell them not to. On one hand, they can taste the feeling of a huge step-change process improvement; on the other hand, they can imagine the feeling of having to park their car and walk through the gate having not been successful.

Lean Learnings: Create an environment where your team is not afraid to fail and you will realize success beyond your wildest dreams. Celebrate their successes with regal fanfare and be willing to hold their hands when they figure out they have to go back to the shop floor and try again.

Before I could get out to the shop floor, Kellen stopped me with a crazed look in his eye.

"You have to slow them down. Scott the maintenance tech is talking about ripping out some main reactor piping and rerouting it."

"Whoa, Kellen, calm down. What's going on?"

Kellen paused for a brief minute to catch his breath and started again. "You are usually in before 6:00 am. What happened today?"

"I had to take care of a bit of paperwork for the team; this morning, Nichole and I went to an early breakfast. I haven't been paying enough attention to her lately."

"Look, I just think we are going to end up making too many changes at once. We need time to process this all. If they find some waste, that's great. We should batch in the changes using a controlled rollout plan. I think we need to get some data on each change first."

"If we do that, it could take a year for us to wrap up one kaizen. I want to have four done this year alone. What is the problem with making a rapid step-change? We need it desperately."

Lean Learnings: Continuous improvement is an excellent strategy if you are already the leader in your industry. It is a terrible strategy if you are lagging behind; those are the times that you need rapid, step-change improvement. Continuous improvement has become something of a buzzword.

"I need data to validate all of the changes. How will we be able to take data on each individual change if we make three or more changes all at once? It would be like trying to hit a moving target!"

"What you are saying makes sense from a classical engineering approach. Let us throttle it back a bit. We can use our enterprise resource planning system to capture the pre-kaizen data for the last several years. We will likely have a thirty-day action item list after the event. So, we will suspend data collection until sixty days after the kaizen. Then we will take a new set of data that we will label as post-kaizen. We will use this to evaluate the success of the event. We shouldn't need more than ninety more days of data to make a determination with a reasonable level of confidence."

"It just seems all too easy. I just don't understand what my role as a process engineer will look like in this new lean organization."

"Your job becomes simpler, not easier. It also becomes more sacred. I saw in the process engineer's report that you were looking for support to put in a better heat exchanger for the main reactor. Is that correct?"

"Yeah it is. It would cut almost an hour of cycle time of our constrained process. No one wants to help me get it done."

"Johnny is not going to learn how to properly size a heat exchanger unless he goes back to school. When he is in the value stream manager role for resin, I bet that he comes and asks you how to heat up the reactor in a quicker and more controlled fashion. In a lean role, you will be an oracle of knowledge. In most organizations process engineers have to manage sideways and a lot of times they are unsuccessful doing so. A friend of mine even went to a class on the subject. This really can be a positive thing for you if you recalibrate your thinking."

"I can't even imagine the front-line team respecting me like that. This has been a tough couple of years for me."

"Hang in there; don't be worried about the kaizen team. We will rationalize the data and your interactions with them. The best solution is for you to volunteer to be on the next team."

"I think I just might. Should I be reading anything to help me out?"

"Yes, the daily operations reports! We need to break down the wall between all the different functions. If you really want to know what you should be doing I will tell you, but I don't know if you are going to like it or not."

"Just tell me - I am curious now."

"Put on a set of coveralls and go make some batches with the third shift. It will do wonders for your relationships on the floor."

"I get what you mean by that, but are you sure it will work? What makes you so sure?"

"I can't guarantee it, but it certainly won't tarnish it. Just go out there with the mind of a three year old. Be polite. Ask good questions and listen to the operators. They know more than you probably think that they know; they have been doing these jobs for twenty or more years."

Leadership Learnings: Your team doesn't have to see you doing their jobs every day; however, they must know that you are willing to! Respect their position and they will respect yours!

Kellen and I parted ways and I made my way out onto the shop floor. I hoped I wasn't too hard on him; I was sincerely hoping that I would catch him off guard wearing a full-face respirator and reacting some resin in a few days or so.

As I made my way over to the kaizen team's base camp, I was awestruck. Off in the distance I saw a mass of yellow, red, and blue stickies covering the south wall. I hurried up and made my way over to the team.

"WOW! That's awesome!"

The team had built four individual process maps based on a simple four-step flow chart.

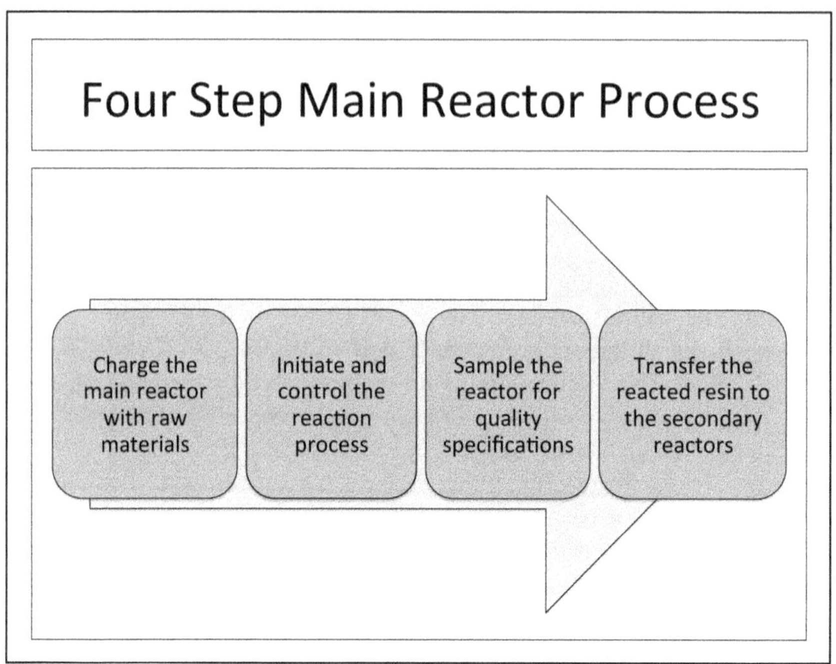

Each map had dozens of sticky notes on the wall.

"Ok…the million dollar question. How many stickies did you end up using?"

"Sir, we would like to have a moment of silence for the many trees who died to make this kaizen possible," Trevor joked.

Daniel poked out his chest and said, "We are definitely at over 200 now."

Enrique said, "We are up to like 240. We haven't finished yet; we still have to map out the transfer process. We will definitely be done by the end of the day today. Johnny is going to teach us about value-added and non-value added activities."

"Plus we have added many more wastes to the Tim Wood forms," Daniel said.

"Very good! I will see you guys up front in a little bit for the debrief."

Day Two Report Out

The team certainly seemed more pumped up today than they were yesterday. They had finished the most important task, which was mapping out the process. Their waste list was three times as long as it was yesterday.

"Alright team, what did you guys learn today? Wait, better question… what did you discover in the process today that you didn't know yesterday?"

Enrique seemed to be extra energetic and said, "We learned that the main reactor production process is really four sub-processes combined together:

1. Raw Material Charge: the operator obtains and segregates the raw materials that are applicable for the next batch and loads them into the main reactor.
2. Initiating Reaction: once the raw material is loaded in the reactor, the operator adds the catalyst and main reactant using the control panel. Once reaction is obtained, the operator monitors reactor instrumentation.
3. Quality Inspection: the operator sends a sample to the lab when directed by the manufacturing order and procedure. If the specifications come back satisfactory, the batch is complete. Otherwise, the operator continues the reaction and resamples the material.
4. Material transfer: once the product has passed QA, the operator transfers the contents of the reactor to the appropriate secondary reactor for further processing."

"Wow that's a lot; so would you say the main reactor operator is a highly skilled employee?"

Scott responded, "Absolutely. I had no idea how much technical knowledge was required to do that job safely and correctly."

"Great, the respect for people's part is crucial! What is the team going to be try-storming tomorrow?"

The room got very quiet. It always does. The building of a process map is a very mechanical task. It has clear inputs and clear outputs. The try-storming process requires ideas, innovation, and application of the waste identified in the process map that was just built.

"Team, you guys are doing a great job. Everyone take home a copy of the wastes that you have identified. Look at it and study it. Tomorrow morning you should have a better idea of what you need to be working on. Think about the waste, think about the process, and think about the impact the removal of each waste will do for you."

We broke for the day and the team started discussing the wastes immediately as they left the room. I heard talking back and forth about how to save five minutes here and twenty minutes there. Johnny hung back for a bit. He fidgeted with a stack of papers that were left in the conference room and finally mustered up the courage to speak.

"I'm getting nervous about this. I hope we can make it work."

"Don't worry. You will. All of the process steps have been identified and you have an appropriate ratio of value-added to non-value added tasks. I'm not kidding when I say this, the map will talk to you. Before you leave today, go look at the big map on the wall. Study the four-step overview and study the rest of the chart. Come back in tomorrow and start working. You will figure it out. I believe in you."

"Ok, I will."

I knew Johnny was having quite a bit of self-doubt. I kept thinking about the goal and about how he would feel if and when he was successful.

23. GO CRUNCH SOME NUMBERS

I stopped by the doughnut shop on my way into the plant. I also grabbed a box of coffee for the team. Day three of the kaizen is generally when the fatigue kicks in. I placed two dozen assorted doughnuts and the coffee on one of the tables in the conference room. I sent Johnny a text message letting him know that we had food for the team.

About four minutes later I heard the team scurrying up the main hallway and enter the conference room; Johnny bypassed the conference room and entered my office.

"I have a question for you."

"You don't have to preface every question with that; we should be beyond that point in our relationship."

He didn't crack a smile, so I immediately sat straight up in my chair and asked, "Is everything ok?"

"I'm scared and I need some help. I'm not trying to punt to you, but I want this to be successful."

"Alright, let's talk it through. Do you have a list of the wastes and how much time each waste in the process occupies?"

Johnny handed me a half crumpled Tim Wood observation form with an extra column listing the time for each waste.

Process: Main Reactor Name: Johnny Date: 2/13

Step	Transportation	Inventory	Motion	Waiting	Over Production	Over Processing	Defects	Description of the Waste	Potential Countermeasures	Time
53				X				Waiting for Reactor to get to temperature	?	180
11			X					Traveling up and down the stairs 18 times for loading the reactor	?	100
36	X				X			Pumping raw materials to a holding tank before transferring to main reactor	Repair flow meter on transfer pump	40
1				X				Waiting for Material Orders When none are ready	?	10
15			X					Operator unable to find tools to close reactor hatch	Collocate tools to station	5
14	X		X					Small quantity chemical workstation 170' from reactor addition	Relocate Station	4

CULTURALKAIZEN TIM WOOD Observation Log Page 1 of 1

"Alright, let's walk through each of the wastes you have identified with your team. Tell me about the process used while waiting to get the main reactor up to temperature."

"Once the main reactor hatch is bolted shut, the operator starts the catalyst injection."

"Where is the catalyst injection started from?"

"The operator has to start the pump from a local control panel by the pump," Johnny responded.

"Is he backtracking a number of times between the pump and the control panel during the start-up process?"

"Yes, the operator had done this three times during our observations. How did you know?"

"Anytime you separate things like this, you will see backtracking. The control must occur at one unified location or we should look at other options such as stationing an operator at the location of the pump."

"That makes sense. That probably cost the operator about ten to fifteen minutes by itself, if we can make it work," Johnny replied enthusiastically. "What about the reaction time; what can we do about minimizing the time there? It seems to be the biggest of our opportunities. After we get to temperature, it will sit there for about four to six hours before we send the first sample to the lab."

"I would agree that is your biggest amount of time, but it is not your biggest opportunity."

"How come?" Johnny replied. "I don't understand. It seems to be staring us right in the face."

"It's all about white space," I replied.

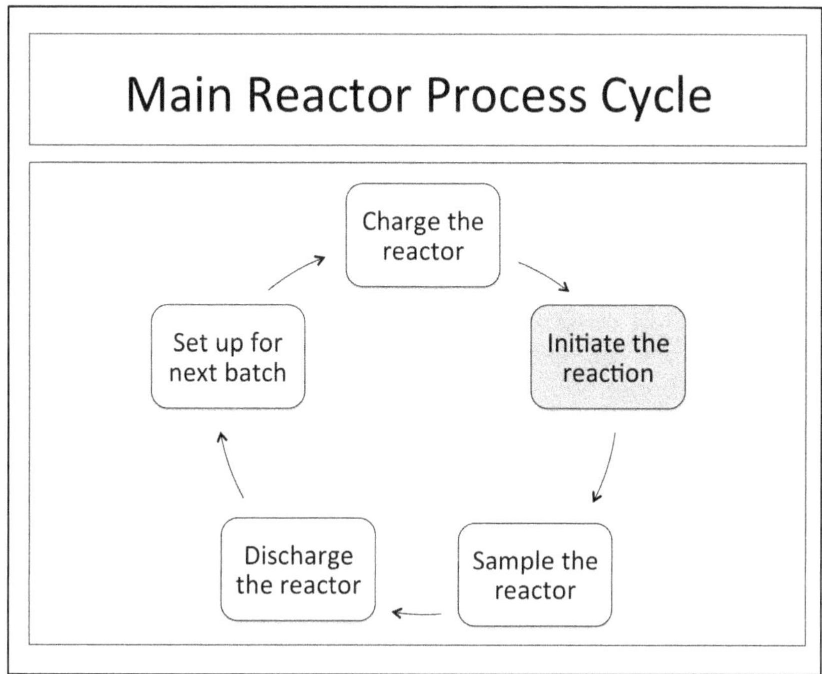

"So the reaction of the process is what is the value-added portion of the production area. Notwithstanding a major process change, there isn't much you can do to improve the efficiency during the reaction. What the kaizen team should focus on is all of the white space that exists between the batches."

Johnny looked a bit puzzled and asked, "So, this 'white space' you are referring to is the setup for the next batch?"

"That's part of it. The white space is all the activities that exist between a batch. Sampling the reactor isn't necessarily a setup activity, but we have to do it before pumping the reactor to a downstream process. If you think about the game of golf, the value-added portion of the golf game is the moment the club strikes the ball. The setup, practice swing, and driving the cart are all white space that exists between the club head striking the ball."

Lean Learnings: In a four hour golf game the golf club is in contact with the golf ball for less than two seconds! Push your team to find all of the process waste that they possibly can. There are, literally, thousands of opportunities to choose from.

Johnny replied, "Wow, that's heavy. So what do I do about the operator traveling up and down the stairs eighteen times while loading the reactor?"

"I hate to answer a question with a question, but what needs to happen? What is wrong with that many trips during the loading process?"

"Well, it's unsafe for them to keep climbing up and down the stairs that many times. It is certainly a great deal of risk. They are going up and down to check flows that are initiated from the control panel and to ensure the material transfer is occurring properly. It's almost like they need another set of hands."

"Ok. Build on that with your team. What's next?"

Johnny said, "The next waste is easy. We pump raw materials to a holding tank before transferring to the main reactor because the flow meter is broken. We weigh the holding tank on a scale and then pump the proper weight to the reactor. We just need to fix the flow meter. Can I spend the money to fix it?"

"Sure, it's a no-brainer."

"Currently, I print all the material orders for the team. What if we trained other people to be able to process material orders instead of just me as the scheduler?"

"That will work. How about the last one?"

"We add some specialty chemicals to the reactor that help control the properties of the resin during reaction. They are currently weighed and stored on the other side of the reaction area. We should locate them closer to their point of use."

"Good, it sounds like you have enough to go start trialing some ideas and collecting some time data."

"Anything else you think I should know?"

"As a matter of fact, there is. I didn't communicate these rules in training, but if you find yourself in need of some help remember these items. They are basically aces up your sleeve in case all other ways to reduce cycle time aren't going as well as you had hoped."

Aces for Reducing Process Cycle Time

- ❑ Synchronize
- ❑ Schedule into multiple processes
- ❑ Minimize handoffs
- ❑ Move steps in the process close together
- ❑ Find and remove bottlenecks
- ❑ Use automation
- ❑ Smooth workflow
- ❑ Do tasks in parallel
- ❑ Consider people as in the same system
- ❑ Use multiple processing units
- ❑ Adjust to peak demand

Adapted From: Langley, G.J., Nolan T., Nolan K., The Improvement Guide : A Practical Approach to Enhancing Organizational Performance. 1st ed. The Jossey-Bass Business & Management Series. 1996, San Francisco: Jossey-Bass Publishers. xxix, 370.

"I don't understand all of these right now."

"That's ok. They *will* make sense when you are on the floor. Remember, being on the floor is where all of the action takes place. You are smarter than you give yourself credit for."

Lean Learnings: We introduce concepts in the classroom; we learn on the shop floor. The shop floor can be anything from a manufacturing site to a customer service representative's cubicle. The shop floor is anywhere value is added for the customer.

"So what do we need to do next?" Johnny asked.

"Follow the schedule; it's day three, so get out there on the floor and try some stuff. If you need any supplies, have Scott talk to Frankie. I have told Frankie to be ready for you and to buy whatever you need as long as it is within reason. If it's over a thousand dollars, come see me and we can still talk about it. Make sure you grab some data; teach your team to time the steps in the process."

"I have never done anything like that before. How am I supposed to teach the team that? Are you sure you shouldn't have led the first one of these events?"

"I'm sure; I'm still an outsider to this place. The change will be more meaningful if it comes from within. You have built relationships with the team. Some are good; some aren't as good. Either way, it is still better coming from you. If it came down to the success of the event, I would have stepped in, but you are absolutely capable. Here is some help for data collection.

Process: ______________ Name: ____________________ Date: ____________

Step	Task	VA	NVA	Trial 1	Trial 2	Trial 3	Trial 4	Trial 5	Trial 6	Average	Comments
1											
2											
3											
4											
5											
6											
7											
8											
9											
10											
11											
12											
13											
14											
15											
16											
17											
18											
19											
20											
21											
22											
23											
24											
	Total Process Cycle Time										

CULTURALKAIZEN TryStorm Observation Log Page ___ of ___

"Just record the time required for each step in your try-storming process. Make sure that you take data on the current state as well. This will enable you to make the proper decisions on how to change the process."

"This isn't complicated; I always thought collecting data was supposed to be in the realm of engineers and mathematicians. I feel like I am missing something."

"You can make it complicated, but it doesn't have to be. There is a time and a place for using some advanced statistical tools, but now is not that time. Get out on the floor and start trying some new stuff. It's already 8:00 am. Let's get busy."

Lean Learnings: It is much easier to teach the concepts of waste, flow, and value than to teach process capability index. Decide what and how much of your team you want involved in process improvements.

"Thanks a lot. Sorry for all the questions. I just don't want to let the team down."

"I know that. It's going to be all good."

Johnny left my office and, much to his surprise, the team was already on the floor. Apparently, Enrique had corralled the team out to the shop floor to begin looking at some new ideas. I was about to settle in to knock out some administrative items that I had been tasked with when Kellen and Sara frantically entered my office.

24. EMAIL BOMB

Kellen and Sara were talking over each other and speaking in short staccato sentences for about two minutes when I finally had to settle them both down.

"Whoa, calm down. What's going on?"

Kellen responded, "Well, we both got a rather mysterious email about half an hour ago and we wanted to come talk to you about it."

"Yes!" Sara interjected. "I wanted to let you know as well. I don't want any more missteps like before."

They both had my curiosity piqued. I had either begun to build a good amount of loyalty or I had two extremely paranoid and high-strung team members.

"I just forwarded you the email," Kellen said.

"I did too," Sara said.

I skimmed the messages that Kellen and Sara had just sent me for a few seconds and it was strikingly obvious that Devon was fishing for information about our site and the kaizen event we were running. The timing was just too perfect to be a coincidence. My instincts told me that I needed to craft a set of responses and carefully deflect any issues he was raising directly or insinuating. That is not leadership with integrity.

"I appreciate the both of you bringing this to my attention; his questions are legitimate. Make sure you respond to his email. He would certainly not appreciate his communication going unanswered."

Kellen and Sara looked puzzled. My perception from this was that the previous person who owned my office *would* have given them a carefully contrived set of answers to respond to Devon's questions.

Kellen waited a few moments before offering, "We both want to present a good case for the plant. Neither of us have ever seen the workers this energized. I have never been a part of any kaizen events. What I do know is that there are six team members out on the floor experimenting and trialing different things to make the process better and repeating a mantra of 'Eliminate all the waste!' This is a good thing and we need more of this, not less. Whatever we need to do to make sure that this process continues, I will certainly support it."

Sara concurred. "Yes, I agree. I have never seen the team happier. They are all thoroughly engaged. We haven't had an injury yet and I see that the team is more engaged. We just want to know what to say, so that our improvement doesn't falter."

"Alright, I get what you are trying to do. I just don't want it to seem staged. Let's go over the questions he sent to you."

----- Original Message -----
From: Devon Carpenter
Sent: 02/14 12:50 PM
To: Kellen
Subject: ACTION REQUIRED: Status Updates

Kellen,

Since you report to my process-engineering group and not directly to the local site, I would like you to provide me an update regarding the status of a few items:

1. What is the status of the process improvement event occurring at your local site? What steps are being taken to ensure we meet our improvement targets for the year?
2. Please explain why you are not directly involved in the process improvement efforts of the site. This is what we are measuring your performance against for the year.
3. Is the proper statistical data analysis being performed during the process improvement?

Regards,

Devon Carpenter
VP of Operations

Kellen asked, "How do I update him on question one?"

"Just tell the truth. We have a process improvement event taking place during this week and we will schedule up to four more kaizen events for the rest of the year. We are tracking monthly process improvement efforts and reporting on productivity as requested."

Kellen responded, "Ok, that's basically what I was going to put for the first one. What about the last two?"

"I would talk about the switch from a vertical to a horizontal organization structure. We want the team driving the process improvements, but not you driving the process improvements. We want you to become a technical *resource* instead of a technical *expert.* It is a subtle difference, but one that is very important. The process engineer should not wear the weight of the world on his or her shoulders; for example, you should not be held accountable for all of the improvements of the plant. What I want to see is team members coming to you with questions about how to eliminate the waste they have found. You will actually become less busy, but more effective. Most of the leg work will be done for you. It is an entirely different way of thinking."

"What about the statistical analysis question? I have to admit, I have been confused by this one as well."

"It is a legitimate point. The changes that the kaizen team will be targeting are mostly simple changes. They all will involve flow and waste. You don't need statistical analysis to tell if we should implement. What we will do is perform a kaizen validation after the event is over. We will analyze the pre-kaizen data and the post-kaizen data. We will determine if the kaizen actually helped. I can't say we will use advanced statistical tools, but we should begin teaching the kaizen leaders how to use confidence intervals and deviations."

Lean Learnings: Generally, it isn't necessary to spend three weeks collecting data to eliminate one of the seven wastes. However, if elimination requires some capital expenditure, you need to make sure the change bears fruit.

"That makes sense," Kellen replied. "I hope it is enough to pacify Devon's line of questioning."

"I wouldn't think of pacification as the right mentality. We are simply using a different methodology to get our improvements. What we will gain by driving the change in the organization up instead of down is the power of time compounding. We will have many small improvements coming from the shop floor instead of one or two large ones driven from the top down."

"I had a very similar set of questions from him. Can we go over them please?"

----- Original Message -----
From: Devon Carpenter
Sent: 02/14 12:58 PM
To: Sara
Subject: ACTION REQUIRED: Status Updates

Sara,

Since you report to the Environmental, Health, Safety & Regulatory department and the local site, I would like you to provide me an update regarding the status of a few items:

1. What is the status of the process improvement event occurring at your local site? Are we ensuring that the process improvements will help us meet our safety targets for the year?
2. Please explain why you are not directly involved in the safety improvement efforts of the site. This is what we are measuring your performance against for the year.
3. Are proper safe change management administration techniques being used to ensure the safe working conditions of the site?

Regards,

Devon Carpenter
VP of Operations

"For the first question, I would just communicate that the focus of all kaizen events is to remove waste. Removing waste from the process limits exposure to all kinds of safety hazards. Also tell him that we are tracking the number of employee safety improvement suggestions. We can't directly correlate the number of safety suggestions to reducing injuries, but certainly having employees more focused on improving plant safety will help increase their awareness of the hazards that exist around them. For the second question, I would explain that by having the improvements come from the front-line worker, we are empowering them to take ownership of their workspace. Again, I want you to be a safety *resource*."

Sara finished scribbling on her pad and said, "What about the corporate change management process?"

"That is actually a very important step that we must integrate into our kaizen system. Properly managing process change is vital to success in a chemical plant environment. George understands the importance of managing this change. We have to very carefully add our corporate policies into the kaizen process. Kaizen is going to tell you to eliminate something that may be 'required waste.' The required waste takes the form of documentation, processing steps, and even raw material introductions. These items are called non-value added, but necessary."

Sara asked, "Won't this slow down our kaizen event implementation?"

"Yes, this is where I get confused. I feel like it will slow us down," Kellen added.

"It can and in many cases should, but that's ok. We can't design our process improvement efforts to prioritize short term rewards over long term problems. You have to consider the application. If we are changing some flows in the warehouse, the corporate documentation is very simple. If we are changing where we want to pipe some highly flammable liquid to, then we want to investigate it carefully. This is where the two of you are used as *resources*. If one of the value stream managers comes to you with a tough question like that, I would expect the both of you to tell them how we can get it done safely or if there is no way that we can make that kind of change. Does that make sense?"

Kellen responded, "It does now. I was feeling kind of left out. I didn't know what my role would end up being."

Sara nodded in agreement.

"That's up to the both of you. You have to decide what you want to do long term. Both of you are strong enough to run a plant one day. My advice to either of you is: figure out where you want to be two, five, and ten years down the road. We can craft a plan around that."

Kellen quickly responded, "Obviously, I want my own plant to run."

"I would recommend that you spend some time as a production supervisor. This will enable you to see the challenges that the production team goes through every day. It will make you a much better site leader in the long run."

Kellen looked puzzled. "How can I be a technical resource from that position? I feel like it is a step backwards career-wise."

"I wouldn't look at it that way. I would like to see every production or operations manager have experience as a front-line supervisor. When you put yourself in that role, you will be directly interfacing with the value-added workers. Also, you will become your own technical resource. You have the technical skills necessary to change things very quickly. The important part is to make sure that the improvement ideas come from the front-line. You will have them on your team if you do it that way. If you play the 'I am the smart engineer' game, you will lose your advantage."

Leadership Learnings: Remember, managing twenty engineers or staff personnel is an entirely different experience than managing twenty front-line associates. Neither is easier or more difficult; they are just different.

Sara replied, "I don't really know yet. I was so close to getting fired last year that I am just happy to have a job."

"Just think about it. Both of you will be in support roles for at least a little while longer. You can absolutely make a difference. I promise."

25. TRY-STORMING SUCCESS?

It was closing in on the end of day three of the kaizen event. The team was gathering in the conference room to give their report out for the day. Their spirit wasn't quite as high as it had been during the two previous days. This is very typical during a kaizen event. The first portion of the kaizen event, mapping out the process, is very mechanical. When the team has taken and analyzed a picture of the process, they feel very certain of success. The team will sometimes hit a wall during the try-storming portion of the kaizen because they realize that they cannot change the entire world in one week. This loss of momentum is predictable; facilitating and leading a kaizen is hard work.

Day Three Report Out

"Ok team, what did you all end up trying today to improve the process?"

Johnny spoke. "We have certainly figured out a great deal of ideas that aren't going to work and a few that we think will."

"That's pretty much how it goes. I should have done this the other day. Let me throw up some information on the try-storming process."

Try-storming Effectively

- Try-storming is where brainstorming meets execution
- The best trystorming is done from the perspective of a three-year-old
- The team must embrace & celebrate their failures
  - When you are failing, you are learning
  - When you are learning, you can innovate

Trevor commented, "What does a toddler's mind have to do with a kaizen?"

"Does anyone have children?"

A few of the team members raised their hands.

"What is the number one question a child will ask you?"

Almost in unison, the team members that had children yelled out, "WHY!"

"Very good. Children always ask why. It's also more than that. Children aren't limited by possibility thinking. Children are natural dreamers. They are also not constrained by the status quo."

Enrique joked, "It sounds like we need to bring the kids to work on the team."

"Just bring their spirit with you. The thing that adults have is knowledge. Couple your knowledge with the mentality of a child and try-storm from that perspective."

I flashed up my next try-storming slide.

Trystorming Process

- Go to the Gemba
- Make a list of potential ideas to remove the identified wastes
  - Evaluate the ideas for feasibility, cost, ease of implementation
- Try the ideas out in real-life applications
- Refine the solution until you get optimal results

"The first step is the obvious one. Get out on the shop floor to make a difference. I saw the team on the shop floor all day long. You guys were effectively engaging the other front-line associates."

Trevor responded, "It was interesting and surprising at the same time. The employees were very receptive because we were asking them, not telling them. They had all kinds of suggestions for us as well. Some of them we incorporated into our ideas."

Daniel said, "We actually trialed some of the items on the list to prove their effectiveness."

"The last step is to refine the solution until you get optimal results. Remember that everything we change is still a work-in-progress. We are never finished improving the process. We have to keep going. We will never be perfect, but we have to keep trying to get there. Alright, so what did you all try-storm today?"

Johnny passed around two forms to everyone in the conference room. The first was the list that we went over yesterday and the second was a try-storming log.

Process: Main Reactor Name: Johnny Date: 2/13

Step	Transportation	Inventory	Motion	Waiting	Over Production	Over Processing	Defects	Description of the Waste	Potential Countermeasures	Time
53				X				Waiting for Reactor to get to temperature	?	180
11			X					Traveling up and down the stairs 18 times for loading the reactor	?	100
36	X				X			Pumping raw materials to a holding tank before transferring to main reactor	Repair flow meter on transfer pump	40
1				X				Waiting for Material Orders When none are ready	?	10
15			X					Operator unable to find tools to close reactor hatch	Collocate tools to station	5
14	X		X					Small quantity chemical workstation 170' from reactor addition	Relocate Station	4

CULTURALKAIZEN TIM WOOD Observation Log Page 1 of 1

Process: Main Reactor Name: Enrique Date: 2/14

Step	#	Description of the Idea	Results
1	1	Crosstrain operators to issue material orders	Operators can generate their own work
14	1	Relocate Small addition station	Trial Successful-Purchased a workstation and relocated small addition station.
15	1	Collocate tools to reactor control station	Helps, but operator still needs tools on top level
	2	Add a second tool station at top level	Will work- Cost of extra tool set is $800
36	1	Repair flow meter	Should work- Cost of repair is $650
53	1	Waiting for Reactor to get to temperature	Kellen & Sara are now evaluating possibility of increasing heating speed safely.
36	1	Try to increase the size of the raw material packaging from 2,000 → 3,000 kgs.	Supplier cannot accommodate change
	2	Install an elevator	Not feasible-Large capital project > $100K
	3	Install bulk equipment for raw materials	Not feasible-Large capital project > $100K
	4	Install an electric hoist	Called manufacturer. Would be $25,000
	5	Subdivide the main reactor area in half; add an additional operator for assistance	

CULTURALKAIZEN Trystorming Idea Log Page 1 of 1

"Wow. That's a big list. The team has had a busy day three."

Scott, who was usually quiet, said, "We have come up with some decent ways of fixing the easy ones on the list. We just need to keep working. I wish we had more time."

"Let's go through the list and we will worry about that later."

Johnny started. "We wanted to knock out the easier ones first. Operators have to wait for material orders sometimes. If the plant scheduler and I are tied up, this could be a good amount of time."

Dave said, "Usually it's only a few minutes, but it has occasionally been several hours!"

Johnny stated, "We are going to cross-train the operators to release the next production order. This way the longest they will have to wait is five minutes."

"Excellent! How come this hasn't been done before?"

Johnny replied cautiously, "Well, honestly, the plant manager didn't want the operators doing it for fear of them making a mistake."

"Ah. This is very typical. I do agree that the operators won't be doing it very often. Make sure you have a good set of visual work instructions that clearly show in words and pictures how to do this. We can't expect the team to remember exactly how to do something they only do once every couple of weeks."

Lean Learnings: Sometimes a 50% solution is good enough! It would have been easy for an experienced manager to tell the team that printing a material order is a non-value added task and then go into a diatribe about visual scheduling and pull systems. The team was not ready for this yet. Respect the team enough to give them the freedom to grow.

Daniel exclaimed, "See! I told you he would let us do it."

Everyone laughed.

"This is your plant. The only questions I am going to ask you are:

1. Is the change safe?
2. Is the change possible?
3. Is there anything about the change that will hinder servicing our customers?

"Other than that, it is all up to the team's decision."

Enrique continued, "The second try-storm was for us to relocate the small chemical addition station. We relocated the scale and chemical storage to the addition location and we trained the operators to the new process. Johnny got the purchasing team to get us a new workstation and we had Frankie rent a small crane to transport it up to the top level."

"This is also a safety win for us. We don't have to carry a container of chemicals up three flights of stairs anymore," Dave said.

Johnny continued, "We looked at putting a set of tools by the work station and it will definitely work, but we need another set to put at the top of the reactor. It is going to be $800 for another set of specialty tools."

"So what are you waiting for? Remember one minute of cycle time on this process is equal to fifty thousand dollars per year of potential revenue. The cost associated with new set of tools is basically irrelevant."

Lean Learnings: Controlling costs is one of the last things managers should focus on. Although, getting more product to the customer will generally decrease your cost per unit.

Everyone seemed to perk up. I had assumed before that the management decisions were based on an Ebenezer Scrooge business model, but the fact that they asked to add an extra set of tools was nothing short of shocking.

Scott went on. "The next item on the list was to fix the broken flow meter. A new flow meter is about $5,000. I think I can get ours going for about $650."

"Hopefully you can get it fixed. If not, I will see what I can do to get us capital to replace the instrument."

Johnny said, "The next one we punted to the support staff. There is a large amount of time waiting for the reactor to get to the proper temperature. Based on our conversation, I realized that the team couldn't tackle it in only a week. We spent a few hours talking to Kellen. He agreed that it was something worth tackling and decided to investigate further."

Kellen, who had previously been sitting in the back of the room quietly, spoke up. "I finally understand what you meant by the term technical *resource.* It is going to take me several months to understand the effects of heating more quickly, but it is certainly something worth investigating."

Johnny reached the last item on the list. "The biggest opportunity for the team is where we are having the most trouble."

"How so? Walk me through your thought process."

"First, Daniel had the idea of increasing the size of the container that the raw materials were supplied in. This would require half the manipulations to load the reactor. The problem was that the supplier couldn't accommodate the change. Second, the team came up with some ideas for getting the material in the reactor that were too large. An elevator or some bulk handling equipment, such as storage tanks, would cost over $100,000. We had the idea of using an electric hoist. That would only be about $25,000, but would still not alleviate all of the trips up and down the stairs."

"I don't think you need to throw money at this problem to solve it. Keep thinking."

"We did come up with the idea with adding an extra body to the reaction unit, but, most of the time, the person will just be standing around."

George said, "We have to get approval from the corporate office to add another body. I realize that you are different and you are willing to spend money on tools, but you simply cannot add another employee without getting approval."

"I agree on that part. What else can the team do?"

Dave added, "I only need a body for about an hour; can we use someone for a little bit of time?"

"It sounds possible. Get back on the floor tomorrow and continue try-storming. Your team is doing well. You will figure it out."

Johnny still looked a bit concerned, but he mustered up some courage to approach the last item. "Tomorrow we will be working on the last item on the list. We have to find a way to help the reactor operator out. Remember the main reactor is *the most* import piece of equipment we have in the plant."

26. CAN I GET AN ANDON PLEASE?

The plant's first kaizen was drawing to a close. Day four was about to start. The team had knocked out some of the wastes of the process, but it was unlikely that the target metrics would be attained without some significant progress occurring today. Any amount of positive change would help because it came from a team internal to the organization; however, we needed a big win to show the entire site what kind of a difference that kaizens can make. Also, we needed a big win to maintain the solvency of the business. It was tough for me to not get out there on the floor and drive the change. I wanted to get my hands dirty and help, but that would not allow the plant to grow. I just had to trust that the kaizen process would work.

Around lunchtime, Johnny and Enrique came into my office and looked concerned.

"We think we have the solution, but we can't necessarily prove it," Johnny declared.

"What do you mean by that?"

Enrique continued, "We are going to use an andon responder to help the operator load the reactor."

Johnny provided the details. "It takes the operator just shy of two hours to load the main reactor due to all of the motion and transportation waste. We just had Dave help Stacy, the regular second shift reactor operator, load the reactor. It seems like we will get it done in about forty minutes."

"That's great. What's the problem?"

"There are two problems actually," Johnny replied. "Normally Dave works first shift, so there will be no one to answer the call. But the biggest problem is that I can't prove that it will be this much faster every single time. We can only get one more data point, at most. I just don't know if we are right. These are two seasoned operators. I need more time."

"Johnny, what do you think?"

"I don't know. I can't make this decision alone. I need more time to investigate."

"We are out of time. I need you to make a decision. Will this help us? Use your gut."

"I know it will. I just can't prove it," Johnny said.

I distinctly remember slamming my hand against the wall and saying, "Then make a change! You are never going to have 100% of the information you need to make a decision. It could take us months to get a statistically significant number of trials. If you both believe this will work, then I will support you. Go and figure out the mechanics behind getting this done."

Leadership Learnings: 70% decision making- If you have 70% of the information, have done 70% of the analysis, and feel 70% confident, then move. A less than ideal action, swiftly executed, stands a chance of success. If you have less information, your chance of success is too low, if you have more – you may have waited too long.

~US Marine Corp Leadership Traits

"Enrique, are you in agreement?"

"This has to work. It just makes sense," Enrique responded. "Two people should be able to perform the process faster than one. The operator has to go back and forth to the control panel many times. Having a second body for the loading process must help."

Johnny and Enrique went back out to the floor. They had about four hours left before the day four report out. They still had a great deal of work to accomplish to get this last change ironed out.

Conversational Interlude

After the team went back out to the floor, I invited George and Steve to have lunch. The kaizen team was anxious to get back out to the floor and left much of the food behind in the conference room. About ten minutes later George and Steve sat down with me.

George broke the ice with the first question. "How do you think everything is going with the kaizen?"

"How about you answer this question first; how do you guys think it is going?"

Steve spoke first. "It seems to be going well. The team is definitely productive, but do you think we will get the results you were looking for? Part of me thinks we should have waited a bit longer. Maybe we should have had more training."

George nodded his head. "Yes, I tend to agree. I hope we didn't go to early. I desperately want this to succeed. The team seems to want it to succeed as well."

"We will just have to wait and see. My gut tells me we did ok. I don't know what exactly would have happened either way. This is the first time I have been involved in supporting a transformation from scratch. There will be many things we get wrong as a leadership team. We will just have to do it better the next time."

George asked, "Do you think the team will get the fifty percent cycle time reduction?"

"I think they will get a significant improvement. It's too early to tell. Once the thirty day action item list is complete, we will validate the data they give to us. It would be foolish for us to think that a twenty percent reduction is a failure. The stretch goals are just that. They stretch your mind out so you aren't constrained to traditional thinking."

Steve asked, "Twenty percent would be huge, right?"

"Twenty percent would be spectacular. My only concern is that the senior management will want to start cutting associate heads to save money," George answered.

"We have to put a priority on service and demonstrate how much more money we can make with the same staffing level. It would be catastrophic to our improvement efforts if that did happen."

Lean Learnings: If the positive results of a kaizen cause the elimination of front-line associates jobs, it will be difficult, at best, to get the front-line team to sign up for another kaizen! Evaluating people's lives on a balance sheet is not respect.

Day Four Report Out

The team walked into the conference room with a bit more bounce in their step. Today we had more visitors than the other three days. Kellen, Sara, Steve, and Frankie were all present, waiting to hear what the team had uncovered during the try-storming portion of the kaizen.

Johnny started off the report. "Today was all about nailing down the solution to the last identified waste. We think we have something that will work. The waste occurs while the main reactor operator is loading the reactor."

"The main reactor operator's job is not generally very labor intensive," Dave continued. "We spend most of our time monitoring the gauges on the control panel. The batch generally takes about twelve hours to complete reaction. We work eight hour shifts, so you may not even load the reactor during your shift. The loading process takes just shy of two hours, so most of us won't start another batch if there is an hour left of shift time."

Everyone was excited to talk about the process. It was obvious that they came up with something good.

Trevor elaborated. "So, this normally low-key job has a burst of high intensity during every start-up. We trialed having Dave help Stacy load the reactor and were able to cut more than half of the load time."

Enrique said, "When the plant started using the material handler andon, it was easy. There was always someone in the material handling role to answer the call."

Daniel chimed in. "Johnny kept saying, 'The main reactor is the constraint; it is the most important piece of equipment in the building. If we can get more through the main reactor, we can get more to the customer.'"

Johnny put up the diagram of the reactor process.

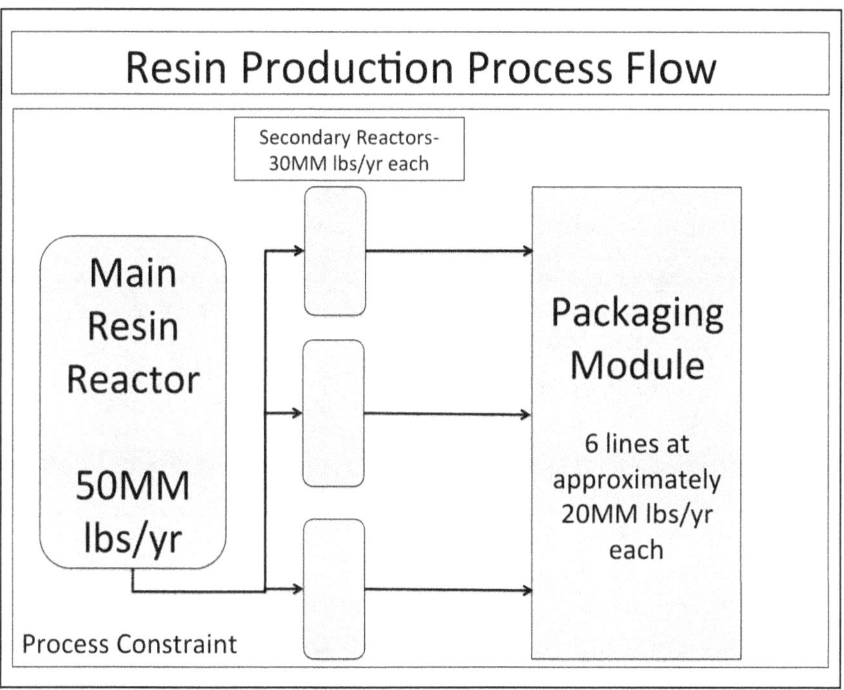

Daniel continued. "We couldn't tell at first why he was talking about that, but then it hit us. If it is the most important piece of equipment, then anyone and everyone should be helping. The packaging line operator or secondary reactor operator could be assigned to help out. For that matter, we could snag a warehouse associate in a pinch. If we are focused on the customer, the top priority is getting the main reactor loaded and reacting again as quickly as possible."

I smiled and said, "That's great, team! So how are you going to signal the responder?"

Scott started explaining their idea. "Initially we will designate an andon responder at the beginning of the shift and issue the responder a radio. The reactor operator will call the andon responder over the radio when it's time to load the reactor."

"What's the long term solution?"

Scott continued with his explanation. "We are going to install seven andon lights and horns at strategic locations around the plant. The reactor operator will initiate the andon light and the responder will answer the call."

"How much conduit do you and the maintenance team have to install?"

Scott replied, "About a thousand feet. It's no big deal. It's obvious that this is important for the success of the plant."

Johnny said, "Once the andon responder arrives on scene, he has a specially designed work instruction for assisting the reactor operator. The reactor operator is running the show with an extra set of hands."

Johnny put up the new and improved idea sheet.

Process: Main Reactor Name: Enrique Date: 2/15

Step	#	Description of the Idea	Results
1	1	Crosstrain operators to issue material orders	Operators can generate their own work
14	1	Relocate Small addition station	Trial Successful-Purchased a workstation and relocated small addition station.
15	1	Collocate tools to reactor control station	Helps, but operator still needs tools on top level
	2	Add a second tool station at top level	Will work- Cost of extra tool set is $800
36	1	Repair flow meter	Should work- Cost of repair is $650
53	1	Waiting for Reactor to get to temperature	Kellen & Sara are now evaluating possibility of increasing heating speed safely.
36	1	Utilize Andon Responder to load reactor	Trial shows reduction of 50% load time

CULTURALKAIZEN Trystorming Idea Log Page 1 of 1

"Excellent work. What kinds of problems did the team face while you were having the kaizen?"

Daniel spoke first. "It seemed like there wasn't enough time. I would basically snap my fingers and it would be time for us to go home."

"Due to the long cycle time of the main reactor process, we weren't able to run as many trials as we had hoped. We had to simulate some different items, but I think we have a made a significant difference," Dave added.

"That's great. It is absolutely appropriate to simulate during try-storming. It is best to have an actual trial, but we work in real-life conditions and sometimes operations will not permit the best-case scenario."

Lean Learnings: The dream state of a culture is to have your entire front-line and management team thinking about how to improve the process all of the time.

Johnny put up the next slide.

Process: Main Reactor Name: Daniel, Trevor & Scott Date: 2/15

Step	#	Description of the Idea	Visual Controls & Standardization Tools
1	1	Crosstrain operators to issue material orders	Create Visual Work Instructions for printing material orders
14	1	Relocate Small addition station	Create Visual Work Instructions for using small adds station & standard replinishment process
15	1	Collocate tools to reactor control station	Create Shadowboard for tools at both workstations
	2	Add a second tool station at top level	
36	1	Repair flow meter	Incorporate meter into maintenance schedule
53	1	Waiting for Reactor to get to temperature	Deferred pending evaluation from tech support
36	1	Utilize Andon Responder to load reactor	Visual Work Instuctions, Visual signals

CULTURALKAIZEN

Johnny continued, "The team made this list of standardization tools that we need to have implemented before the action items are complete. We basically want the whole factory to 'talk' to us. In addition to creating visual work instructions for the changes we are making in the kaizen, one of our action items will be to create visual work instructions for the entire main reactor area."

"I can see value in visual work instructions for maintenance as well. Training a new maintenance technician would be substantially easier with good training aids," Scott said.

"You are absolutely correct, Scott. This can help all processes!"

Lean Learnings: Standard work is the "secret sauce" of truly lean organizations. Many companies overlook this important tool. If you did nothing else but standardize your processes, your results will improve significantly!

"We had the team draft a visual work instruction for one of the simpler processes so we could share the concept with the entire front-line team," said Johnny.

He passed out several copies of a laminated visual work instruction for the team to review.

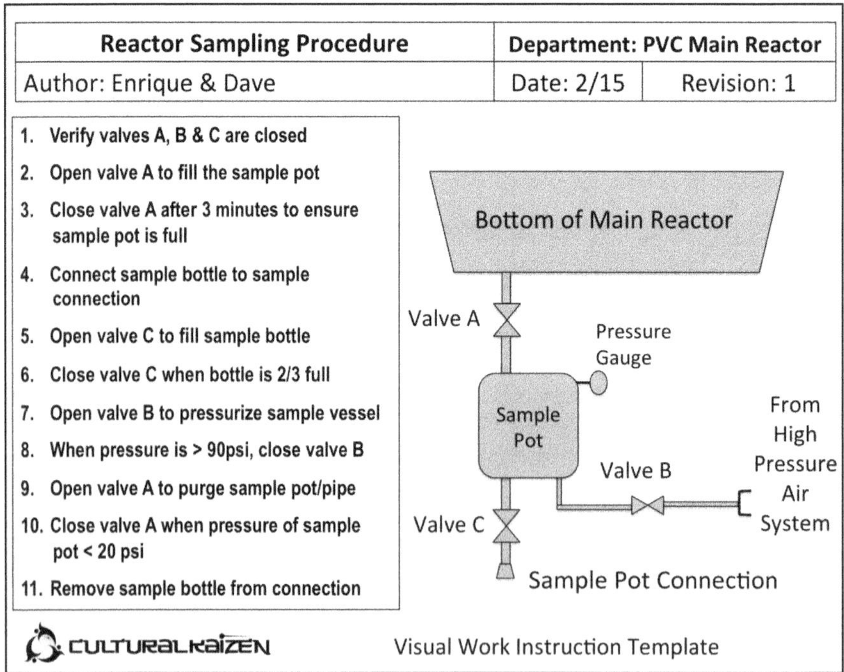

Reactor Sampling Procedure	Department: PVC Main Reactor	
Author: Enrique & Dave	Date: 2/15	Revision: 1

1. Verify valves A, B & C are closed
2. Open valve A to fill the sample pot
3. Close valve A after 3 minutes to ensure sample pot is full
4. Connect sample bottle to sample connection
5. Open valve C to fill sample bottle
6. Close valve C when bottle is 2/3 full
7. Open valve B to pressurize sample vessel
8. When pressure is > 90psi, close valve B
9. Open valve A to purge sample pot/pipe
10. Close valve A when pressure of sample pot < 20 psi
11. Remove sample bottle from connection

Visual Work Instruction Template

George spoke up. "Wow, that's impressive. It is very simple. How did the team like it?"

Trevor responded, "Well, we wanted to give it the best test possible. We gave the work instruction to Glenn, one of the second shift warehouse personnel, and he was able to take a sample by himself. Don't worry, George, we had Dave watching him the entire time."

"That's great. I have wanted nothing more than to cross-train the entire plant," George said. "We have had some instances where we were not able to make product because the only skilled operator was on vacation. This will make training so much simpler."

Steve finally said what was on everyone's mind. "So how are the kaizen targets shaping up?"

Final Kaizen Event Target Sheet

Event Description (work center)	Event Dates
Main Reactor Product A- 60% of volume	2/12-2/16

	Current	Target	Day 1	Day 2	Day 3	Day 4	Final	% Δ
Cycle time (Hours)	12	6	12	12	11	9.5	9.5	21%
Volume per day								
Space (sq. ft.)								
Inventory								
Walking distance								
Transport distance								
Changeover time	2	1	2	2	2	0.6	0.6	70%
Quality improvements								
Visual controls	0	2	0	0	1	6+	6+	
Safety improvements			Reduced Ladder Usage 90%					

CULTURALKAIZEN Kaizen Event Target Sheet

Johnny said, "This isn't quite what you guys were looking for in terms of success, but we did make a significant improvement. The numbers reported are very conservative."

"I like the fact that you reduced the ladder usage so much," Sara confided. "Slips, trips, and falls are the leading cause of injuries in our company. Its use isn't totally eliminated, but the team has significantly reduced our exposure."

"To be perfectly honest, I find myself rushing on the last couple trips up and down. With only one set of trips now, I will be less inclined to rush," Dave acknowledged.

Johnny delivered the financial impact. "The team has saved 150 minutes of cycle time. That is over $10,000,000 worth of capacity."

"That hardly seems possible. We are just a bunch of regular guys." Trevor's tone was a mix of awe and pride.

"We all are a bunch of regular people. What is irregular is that we focused six people on the specific goal of eliminating waste."

"It's safe to say we killed Tim Wood, right?" asked Daniel.

"Tim Wood has a way of creeping back in when we least expect him. That is why we *must* standardize our processes. Remember, the numbers Johnny are quoting are capacity numbers. What we are doing is pushing the constraint onto the market place."

"It's not just capacity! Our service level will improve as well. You have no idea how distracting it is answering phone calls from irate customers," Steve poignantly added.

"I agree. This is excellent work! What are our next steps?"

"Tomorrow, we will finish as much of the standardization as possible, generate our 30-day action item list, and communicate our results and plan to the rest of the plant," Johnny replied.

"Wonderful. Does anyone have any questions?"

Trevor quipped, "Where are we going to eat?"

"Anywhere the team wants! Just let me know."

The team started to migrate out of the room. Kellen hung back for a second.

"I'm sorry if I didn't seem supportive at first," Kellen apologized. "I had no idea the power of the using this methodology. There are kaizen team members that wouldn't help me at all when I was trying to get some traction for process improvements."

"It all boils down to respect. All people are worthy of our respect."

"I think I might want to work in a production supervisor role for a year or so. I see now how it could benefit my development."

"We will talk about it. In the meantime, you and Sara have a large action item to work on. Do you think you can reduce the heating time?"

"We are going to give it our best shot; I know we have a team of people on the floor that will support us as well."

"Good. Now you are learning to see."

27. FINAL REPORT OUT

We gathered in the conference room for one final message from the team. There were many conversations going on in the background. People were all anxiously waiting for the presentation from the kaizen team. It was hard to believe that all this enthusiasm had been generated in less than four months. As the plant team finished gathering in the room, the kaizen team went up to the front of the room. I noticed a positive spirit in all of them before they even spoke.

Johnny dimmed the lights and fired up the projector.

Kaizen Team Selection

1. Johnny- Production Supervisor- **Team Lead**
2. Enrique- Lab Tech **Co-Lead**
3. Dave- 1st shift Main Reactor Operator
4. Daniel O- 2nd Shift Solvent Operator
5. Trevor-1st Shift Warehouse Operator
6. Scott M- 2nd Shift Maintenance Tech

Johnny addressed the crowd. "Everyone knows the kaizen team by now. We sat down about a month ago to pick the best structured kaizen team that we possibly could. We used a cross-functional approach for team selection. Our mentality was that we wanted a composite of experience from the plant to give us a fresh set of eyes on the process."

Area of Focus
❑ Main reactor selected as target area ❑ The main reactor was chosen because: ❑ It is the process constraint of our most profitable product ❑ We have excess demand due to superior product quality ❑ Demonstrated lead time is close to a month in some cases

"The scope of the kaizen was directed toward the main reactor," Johnny said.

"The principal behind the kaizen was: if we can get more material through the main reactor by eliminating Tim Wood, then we can get more product to the customer," Dave said proudly.

George whispered to me while Dave made a few more points. "Wow! He really does get it. I'm kind of ashamed to admit that I didn't think they would be able to."

"That's ok. We are all growing in different ways."

Dave continued, "We need to develop extra capacity on our main reactor because we cannot get our resin to the customer as effectively as we need to."

Trevor said, "There have been cases where I am picking orders for drums that are six weeks old."

Direct Observation to Define Current State

- ❑ Team members were assigned to different roles to document every facet of the process
- ❑ Specialized jobs were given to each team member to increase process effectiveness
- ❑ The goal of the first two days of the event was to know the process inside and out

Enrique said, "The first part of the kaizen is to do an in-depth study of what is actually going on in the floor. We split the team members up into very specific job functions for this. Dave, the only reactor operator on the team, served as our process pilot."

"My job was to basically be a tour guide for the team. I was showing the team how the process was running before the kaizen. Enrique was our scribe. He took down every single step of the process as we were walking through the reaction area."

Trevor said, "I was the surveyor. I sketched out a diagram of the process and traced out the flows of information, people, and materials. It is called a spaghetti diagram because it literally looks like a plate of spaghetti noodles when you are finished!"

"I assisted Trevor by calculating the distances traveled between steps," Johnny said. "Daniel and Scott had the most important job of all. They were our spotters. They identified the sources of waste as we came across them."

"By mapping out the process we figured out that there are four basic phases to the main reactor process," Enrique said. He pulled out the next slide.

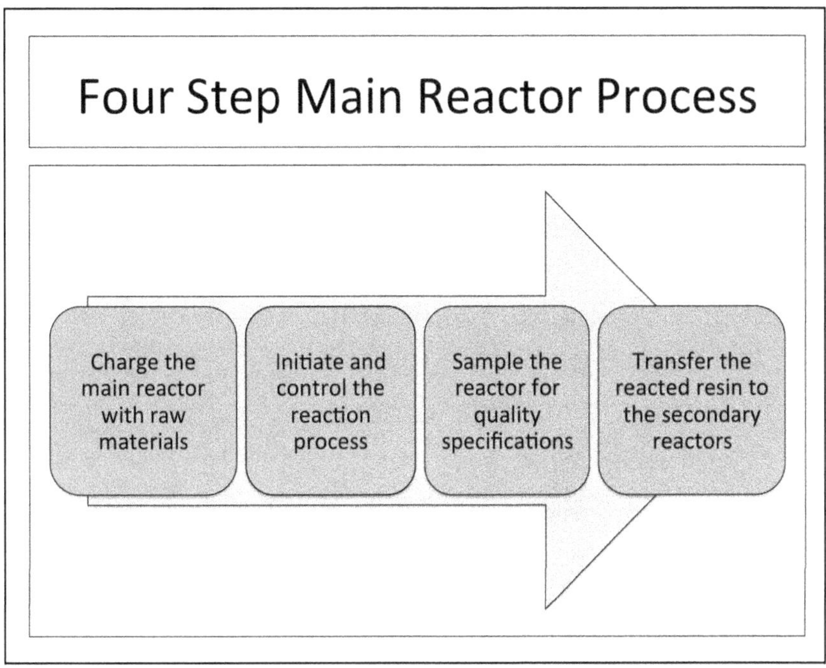

Enrique quickly rattled off the steps. "Here they are:

1. Loading the raw material into the reactor.
2. Initiating and controlling the reaction process.
3. Sampling the reactor.
4. Transferring the contents of the reactor to the secondary reactors."

Clarence, the most senior employee on site, asked, "It's only four steps? I thought I saw you out there with about a million yellow stick-ems up on the wall."

"You are right," Trevor acknowledged. "Each one of these main processes had about seventy to eighty steps each. That's how we identified all of the waste. All of the work instructions for the process had about twenty steps, but they didn't explain what was really going on out there."

Daniel took over. "After we mapped out the process, we spent about three hours identifying all of the wastes in the process. We came up with a list of six major wastes. There are many more than that in the main reactor process, but these were the ones we looked at for this kaizen."

Major Wastes Identified

- ❑ Waiting for the reactor to get to temperature
- ❑ Traveling up and down the stairs from the reactor mezzanine during loading
- ❑ Pumping liquid raw materials to the holding tank to weigh before injection
- ❑ Waiting on material orders
- ❑ Operators looking for tools every batch
- ❑ The small chemical weigh station is too far away

Johnny said, "The first and biggest opportunity we found was the time it took the reactor to get to temperature. Unfortunately, there isn't much we could do with it during a week-long event. Fortunately, Kellen and Sara have agreed to help us out with this one. More to come on that."

Dave tackled the second waste. "I never realized in all my years working here that traveling up and down the stairs that many times could be avoided. It just didn't occur to us that there was a better way. We are going to use a two-person system to load the main reactor. We will designate an andon responder to help with loading the reactor. Using the second person will allow us to cut the time loading in more than half."

Scott continued with the report. "For as long as I have been here, we were using the temporary holding tank to pump the material to pump raw materials to before pumping them to the main reactor. We were doing this because the flow meter was broken. Frankie, the maintenance manager, and I got it fixed last night. It only cost us about $650 in parts to make the repair. Frankie suggested last night to just remove the tank and scale."

Johnny nodded his head in agreement and said, "That tank is about 800 gallons. That will save us additional floor space. That's a good idea!"

"There are many times when the operators start their day that they don't have access to material orders," Daniel said. "We can't be expected to work without them. We designed a process so that operators can generate their own work in a pinch. We will be training the reaction operators to do this over the next week or so."

Dave jumped in at this point. "The next one is, to me, the easiest on the list. How many times have you been looking for a tool and not able to find one?"

About three quarters of the room raised their hands and the rest of the team shook their heads.

"We set up fixed locations for all the tools necessary to run the reactor. Frankie got us an entire additional set of tools to put on the top level of the mezzanine. We are making up a tool board so that we always have everything when we need it."

Enrique spoke next. "The last one is similar to the tool situation. The small chemical addition station was located next to the secondary reactors. We purchased an additional storage station and scale and located it on top of the mezzanine. This is where the addition is made, so the chemicals should be measured there. It is not safe for operators to carry containers of chemicals up the stairs."

Sara commented to me, "Wow! I never expected them to put a focus on safety like that."

"It goes both ways. If we respect them, they will respect themselves. Why wouldn't people want a safe work environment? The only reason is because bad managers hang their jobs over their heads. In the short term people need money to survive."

Johnny began his wrap up. "So what kinds of improvements do you all think we got? How many extra batches do you think we can make, per year, while doing less difficult work?"

"Ten."

"Fifteen."

"I bet twenty or thirty."

"Oh come on, you aren't even close."

Johnny smiled and put up the last slide.

Kaizen Results		
	Before Kaizen	**After Kaizen**
Cycle Time (hours)	12 Hours	9.5 Hours
Batches Per Year	500	631
Average Revenue per Batch	$80,000	
Total Capacity Increase	$10.4M	

Clarence spoke up again. "How is buying extra tools and moving some stuff closer going to do that much? It doesn't seem feasible!"

Trevor responded to Clarence. "We didn't just move some things closer. We systematically found waste in the process and are working to eliminate it."

Dave continued Trevor's thought. "Clarence, there is so much waste left; I bet we could get it down even further if we did another kaizen. Someone like you would find waste that we missed."

Lean-Leadership Learnings: Change management is effortless when the change is coming from the front-line up. The front-line will sell the changes to their peers!

Johnny said, "Over the next thirty days, the team will be implementing these action items along with a few others to solidify these gains. The bottom line is that we need to service the customer better to stay competitive."

"Everyone knows that they have talked about closing this place for many years. If we can do enough kaizens, it won't make sense for them to close it," Dave added.

Doug, a first shift packaging operator, asked, "That's great, but when can we kaizen the packaging line? I have all kinds of problems over there. I hate working when the line isn't running well."

Sammy, a solvent adhesive operator, countered, "Wait, I realize that resin makes the money for the company, but we need help too!"

Johnny looked at me. "When are we having another kaizen event?"

"This plant is all of yours; when do you want to have it again?"

"Can we have one every month or so?" someone asked.

"I think that's a good number. Let's shoot for forty-five days out."

The room started to clear out except for the kaizen team and a few managers. We huddled up one last time.

Steve started the conversation. "Johnny, you guys did a great job. I am totally impressed. I have had classroom lean and kaizen training, but nothing would have led me to believe that we would have these kinds of results. Our customers will thank all of you in the long run."

Trevor said, "I actually had a really good time this week. It was a tough week for me, anyways. I don't know how the rest of the team felt."

"I agree. I am mentally drained. I haven't thought this hard in my entire life. It was definitely a positive experience," Daniel added.

"Everyone did an excellent job on all fronts. Kaizen week is a tough week; it is also a good week! I hope everyone learned something and will help us continue to improve. I think we should use a daisy chain model for training kaizen leaders."

I went over to the white board and sketched out the following:

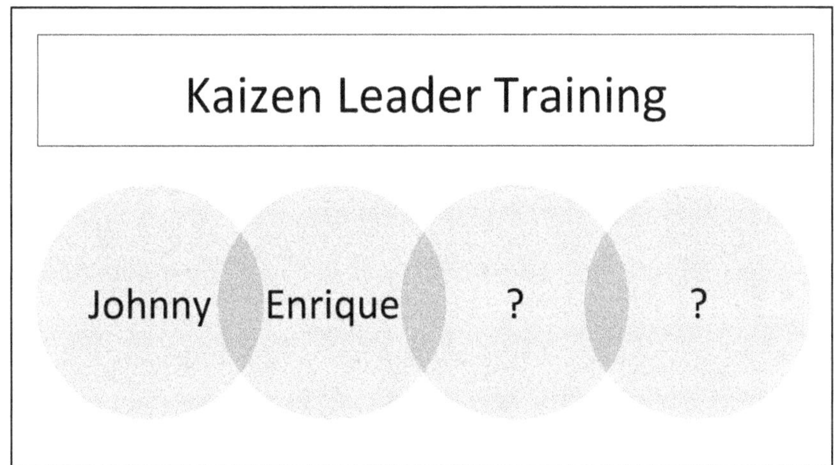

Daniel said, "I'm confused; what do the circles mean?"

"Excellent question. Johnny was the leader of the first kaizen with Enrique as the co-lead. So, Enrique will be the leader of the second kaizen and will pick a new co-leader."

"That makes sense," Johnny said.

Enrique looked a little bit overwhelmed at the prospect. "I dunno if I am ready for that yet."

"You are. I promise. Remember, map out the process, identify the waste, try-storm counter measures, and sustain. That's it!"

Trevor quipped, as usual, "I know what I'm ready for…food!"

Everyone laughed. It had been a good week!

"Where are we going?" I asked.

Dave spoke up and said, "We want to go to the all-you-can-eat buffet at the casino down the highway!"

"Nice! Let's go."

28. GEMBA WALK…ONE YEAR LATER

As usual, I put on my hardhat and safety goggles before making my trip out onto the floor. I swung by the solvent adhesive line and the first thing I noticed is that it was down.

Henry, another production supervisor, was in a group with four other associates. One of the line workers was leading an A3 project, a system of problem solving developed by Toyota.

"So, the sensors on the end of the packaging line are failing constantly. We have been dealing with this for many years. I stopped the line so we could fix it for good."

"I'm going to go get one of the maintenance techs; I think we will need some technical support for this one," one of the team members commented.

I would later find that the root cause of the sensor problem was that they were drifting slightly over time because the machine was vibrating. The team's solution was to add some rubber washers to isolate the sensors from the machine and use a nylon locking nut instead of a standard steel nut. This was literally a one-dollar solution to a problem that caused hours of downtime per week.

Lean Learnings: You do not need money to improve your processes; you need an engaged team willing and able to solve problems.

I gave Henry the thumbs up and continued on my walk. It was interesting to see the A3 being led by the line associate. About three weeks earlier we had given A3 training to the entire team. The whole team's focus had shifted from using a "work-around and limping along" approach to a much better "shut it down and fix the problem" approach.

After I left the solvent line, I swung by the lab. Enrique had just been made the laboratory group supervisor for our division and was very proud.

"Hi Enrique! Congratulations on your promotion."

"Thanks so much," he said. "I don't think I would have made it without the team's help and exposure to kaizen."

"What do you mean?"

"Well, I had to go through a significant number of interviews up at the corporate office in Minneapolis. I had five different interviews."

"Yeah, I know the feeling. My interview for this job lasted all day long. So, how did being a kaizen leader help you interview?"

"It just helped me think about things in a different way. I used to get stuck when interviewers would ask me problem-solving questions. This time I would just map out the answer to the question in my head like I was trying to identify waste during a kaizen."

"Very good. Remember, as managers our success depends upon the success of our team, not our own technical ability. What are you working on anyways?"

"Actually, I was about to call a meeting. I have been running a trial of coating the inside of the lab reactor with Teflon®. I think we can get an extra year or so of runtime between cleanouts if we do this."

"What made you think of that?"

"The team and I were talking about it during lunch a few weeks ago during the cleanout. We had like thirty contractors onsite. We could have been making product for the customer. It was two and a half weeks of pure wasted time plus money for the contractors' services."

Leadership Learnings: "Furthermore, we've found that contrary to what many CEOs assume, leadership is not really about delegating tasks and monitoring results; it is about imbuing the entire workforce with a sense of responsibility for the business."

~Amar, Hentrich & Hlupic, Harvard Business Review 12-2009

"That's amazing. How much would it cost us to get it coated?"

"About $40,000."

"Wow. That's nothing. We spent about $250,000 cleaning out the reactor last time. And we do that every eighteen months or so."

I left the lab with a bittersweet feeling. The team was progressing to a point that they didn't need me anymore. They had become autonomous and extremely productive. It was incredible that they had come so far in just over a year.

I walked over to the warehouse. There were eight sets of shipping lanes freshly painted on the floor. Six of the sets of lanes were staged for outgoing shipments. I noticed Trevor off in the distance explaining to a new associate how to stage shipments in each of the lanes; he was referencing a set of visual work instructions for the process.

Steve saw me and hurried over.

"Did you hear what happened?" he asked.

"Yeah, I did. Devon chose to seek other employment opportunities."

"What are your thoughts on that?"

"Well, I am a little bit sad."

"Really; why is that?"

"'Cause we ended up hitting every single one of his metrics last year and I never sent him an updated spreadsheet."

We both laughed.

I continued, "I really don't know how I feel. I mean I would certainly like to move on in my career, but I would miss working with the team here. On the other hand, the plant may grow more if there is someone else in the role."

"Well, whatever happens, we will all be here to support you."

"I know. Just make sure the place keeps learning, growing, and changing."

As I made my way back to my office, I heard someone training a new associate.

"Tim Wood is waste. We have to get him out our plant…"

APPENDIX A: 5-DAY KAIZEN EVENT SCHEDULE

I have included the kaizen schedule for your convenience here. Remember, all of the processes described in this book are a guide. There is no prescriptive way to introduce lean into a company. A leader looking to use lean as a system for improvement must make an assessment of the organization. Each organization is like a snowflake; they all have a unique culture, strengths, weaknesses, and opportunities. There will never be a lean checklist that will apply to every organization ubiquitously.

Kaizen Roadmap: Day 1

Time	Monday
6:00	Intro, Agenda & Target Sheet/Opportunity
6:30	
7:00	Gemba Walk: Process Overview
7:30	
8:00	Map Out The Process & Identify Wastes
8:30	
9:00	
9:30	
10:00	
10:30	
11:00	Lunch
11:30	
12:00	Map Out The Process & Identify Wastes
12:30	
1:00	
1:30	
2:00	
2:30	
3:00	Action Plan & Report Out

Day 1 Milestones

- ❑ Gemba walk
- ❑ Team assignments for creating process map
- ❑ Begin creation of process map
- ❑ Begin identifying wastes
- ❑ Develop action plan for day 2
- ❑ Prepare report out from day 1

CULTURALKAIZEN

Kaizen Roadmap: Day 2

Time	Tuesday
6:00	Review Action Plan
6:30	Map Out The Process & Identify Wastes
7:00	
7:30	
8:00	
8:30	
9:00	
9:30	
10:00	
10:30	
11:00	Lunch
11:30	
12:00	Identify & Trystorm Countermeasures to Identified Wastes
12:30	
1:00	
1:30	
2:00	
2:30	
3:00	Action Plan & Report Out

Day 2 Milestones

- ❑ Complete process map
- ❑ Complete waste identification
- ❑ Begin identifying countermeasures to discovered wastes and try-storming solutions
- ❑ Develop action plan for day 3
- ❑ Prepare report out from day 2

CULTURALKAIZEN

Kaizen Roadmap: Day 3

Time	Wednesday
6:00	Review Action Plan
6:30	Trystorm Solutions
7:00	
7:30	
8:00	
8:30	
9:00	
9:30	
10:00	
10:30	
11:00	Lunch
11:30	
12:00	Trystorm Solutions
12:30	
1:00	
1:30	
2:00	
2:30	
3:00	Action Plan & Report Out

Day 3 Milestones

- ❑ Identify countermeasures to discovered wastes and try-storm solutions
- ❑ Develop action plan for day 4
- ❑ Prepare report out from day 3

CULTURALKAIZEN

Kaizen Roadmap: Day 4

Time	Thrusday
6:00	Review Action Plan
6:30	Trystorm Solutions
7:00	
7:30	
8:00	
8:30	
9:00	
9:30	
10:00	
10:30	
11:00	Lunch
11:30	
12:00	Develop Plan for Implementation and Standardization
12:30	
1:00	
1:30	
2:00	
2:30	
3:00	Action Plan & Report Out

Day 4 Milestones

- ❑ Complete Try-storming process
- ❑ Begin developing a plan for implementation and standardization of the changes generated from the kaizen
- ❑ Develop action plan for day 5
- ❑ Prepare report out from day 4

CULTURALKAIZEN

Kaizen Roadmap: Day 5

Time	Friday
6:00	Review Action Plan
6:30	Complete Standardization & Implementation Plan
7:00	
7:30	
8:00	Roll-out Results
8:30	
9:00	
9:30	
10:00	
10:30	Celebrate
11:00	
11:30	
12:00	
12:30	
1:00	OFF
1:30	
2:00	
2:30	
3:00	

Day 5 Milestones

- ☐ Roll-out Results of kaizen event
- ☐ Celebrate success with the team

CULTURALKAIZEN

APPENDIX B: GLOSSARY

5 Whys	Approaching a problem by asking why until a root cause is found (five is an arbitrary number).
5S	Toyota production system of process cleanliness and organization. There are many iterations of this, but the five loosely translate to: • Sort • Straighten • Shine • Standardize • Sustain
7 Wastes	A breakdown of the seven types of wastes that exist in our workplaces (and homes).
8th Waste	An eight waste was discussed after the initial seven wastes were discussed. The eight waste is underutilized (not respecting) people.
Andon	Japanese term for light. Used as a signal for assistance.
Capacity	The maximum amount a production process is capable of producing.

Changeover Time	The amount of time required to set a process up to produce a different product.
Constraint	A limiting factor in a production process. The production process isn't capable of producing more than the process constraint is capable of.
Cycle Time	The amount of time required to complete one process from start to finish. Sub-processes can have their own cycle times that add up to the overall cycle time.
Gemba	Japanese term that literally translates to "the real place."
Kaizen	Japanese term that means change for the good.
Kaizen Event	A process improvement workshop that typically focuses on the rapid improvement of a single process. The planning cycle takes three to six weeks and the workshop is generally five days.
Kanban	Japanese term which means "to replenish." System which utilizes authorizations to start the next production lot.
KPI	Key performance indicator: Targets that managers set for performance evaluation. This is often done incorrectly.
Lead time	The time required from receipt of order until the customer receives the product.
Spaghetti Diagram	An overhead map created to show the flow of man, materials, and information.
Standard Work	The development of controls for tasks to create standardized jobs for the purpose reducing variation.

Spaghetti Diagram	A process diagram that shows a birds eye view of the process. It shows the travel of the information, people and materials through a process. It is colloquially called a spaghetti diagram because the overlapping of flows resembles spaghetti.
Throughput	The rate which work moves through an production process.
Value Stream Map	Visual diagram of the process used to show flow from the organization’s supplier to the customer. The value stream map is used to help identify wastes in the process.

ABOUT THE AUTHOR

Paul Swaney has been working in the operations management field since the late 1990s. He has worked in many different manufacturing and operations arenas, such as nuclear energy, refining, petrochemicals, specialty chemicals, plastics, and multiple distribution channels.

He has direct experience as a plant manager for a specialty chemical manufacturing site. Although the characters in this text are fictional, the principles have been applied in real-life situations.

Paul loves everything about continuously improving the process and building people. He believes there is massive potential locked inside every single one of us; we just need the right leader to unlock the magic.

Paul's newest passion is helping other leaders grow their teams and adding value to their businesses. Please visit www.culturalkaizen.com for more information on process improvement and leadership development services provided.

Follow me on twitter @CulturalKaizen

Email: paul@culturalkaizen.com

www.ingramcontent.com/pod-product-compliance
Lightning Source LLC
Chambersburg PA
CBHW051212170526
45166CB00005B/1859

* 9 7 8 1 4 7 5 2 8 4 5 1 5 *